Every Manager's
Lean / Six Sigma
Quick Reference and Toolkit

For Optimum Performance

David Connaughton

ISBN-13: 978-1499270808
ISBN-10: 1499270801

To the many who work
to get the kinks out of
production everywhere

Contents

Available CD ROM Supplement

Many of the tools referenced in this book can be obtained in ready-to-apply form on a CD or via electronic download from ROI-Team, Inc., at ROI-Team.us. In addition, the CD ROM contains PowerPoint slides summarizing each chapter, for reference or for training purposes.

The tools are written in Microsoft Excel for the PC, which includes the capability to create 'Macros,' built-in code that automates actions on spreadsheets (using the Visual Basic for Applications, or VBA programming language). This code DOES NOT RUN ON APPLE 'NUMBERS'.

CD ROM Contents

01	5S Audit	What kind of mess have they made?
02	Prioritizing Tools	What should we work on first?
03	Operations Analyses	What's broken?
04	Kaizen Events	Let's make quick work of it!
05	Process Map	Should we be doing it this way?
06	Throughput - Yield	Does it help to make more?
07	Insource / Outsource	Should we make it ourselves?

The MS Excel files listed here contain the tables and tools illustrated and described in this book. Most are unprotected or protected without a password (leave the password entry field blank) so that you can modify them as needed.

Acknowledgements

This book is an extract from ***It IS Broke The Comprehensive. Fix It! Business Improvement Toolkit***, so the acknowledgements are again of my many friends and acquaintances among the ranks of hands-on consultants and business executives. Especially noteworthy are the late Hans-Peter von Sicard, a consultant's consultant and mentor to many; the well-known lean author and expert Dr. Bill Lareau, who writes books like others write e-mails; Roger Kaufman of Implementation Services, who is a role model for how entrepreneurs should drive and persevere; Dr. Neil Parmenter, Dean of the Business School at Daniel Webster College; Bob Carlson, the chief content editor as the work progressed over the years; and a list of colleagues too numerous to name here but greatly appreciated nonetheless.

Thanks to my wife Marilyn for her support and occasional proof-reading, to the investors of ROI-Team, Inc., whose trust and patience have generated a business rationale for this work, and to my many students who provided so many opportunities for improvement. All these have helped create whatever in this book is useful and accurate; any errata can be attributed directly and solely to the author.

About the Author

David Connaughton is an international management consultant and business school adjunct professor with a long-running passion for operational excellence. He is a graduate of the United States Air Force Academy and the Harvard Business School and resides in Windham, New Hampshire.

Using This Book

Elevator Pitch

Many pages of this text include a very brief synopsis of the material, useful when the CEO catches you on the elevator and asks, "What is this thing called…?" Being good counts most if you also look good!

Step-by-Step

Many of the tools and techniques covered in this book benefit from an organized approach to execution. When called for, this step-by-step sidebar outlines that approach.

You may wish to study this book in detail as a course or use it as a handy reference describing virtually every concept and tool used by successful entrepreneurs, executives and general managers, and Lean and Six Sigma masters. Sources and additional suggested reading are at the back of the book.

The available CD- ROM by ROI-Team follows this text with illustrations, examples and ready-to-use tools in Excel format.

Introduction

In the late 1970s America and Western Europe were unprepared for the invasion of high-quality low-cost 'Six Sigma' producers from Japan, soon joined by others in the Far East that drove electronics and automobiles manufacturing offshore and put Western flagship producers on the ropes. Today every manufacturer in a competitive industry (namely, everyone) needs to apply Lean and Six Sigma principles to stay in the game. This book is intended to make that a little easier for both the companies and the individuals that make them up.

This book is about efficiently producing anything to meet the quality requirements of whoever pays – customer, investor, philanthropic supporter, or government entity, for examples – of goods including durable items, paperwork transactions, hardware of all types, and software, for examples. A whole set of concepts, tools, and techniques have been developed to support these quality and efficiency requirements, and in most organizations and industries they are not optional. It is useful to group these concepts under 3 complementary disciplines: Lean, Six Sigma, and Agile Development.

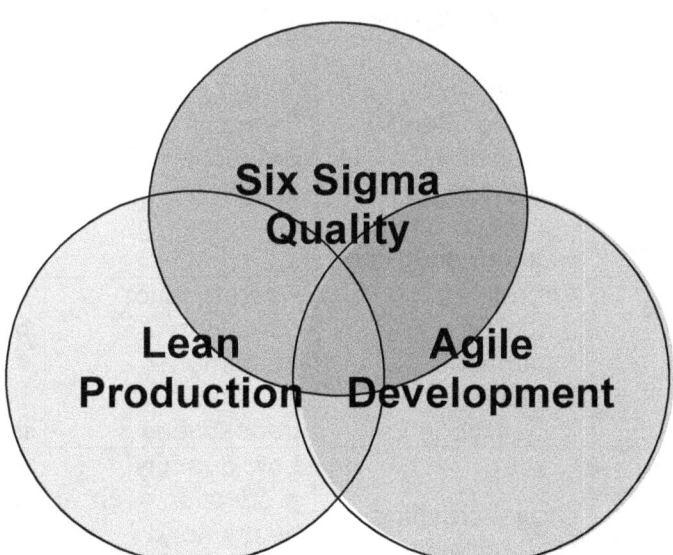

Depending on the product or service produced, each of these disciplines may be of greater or lesser importance, as suggested in the chart on the next page. Regardless of the type of operation, however, producing what the customer

Introduction

demands in a timely manner at an affordable cost is always required for survival and growth.

Six Sigma addresses quality, defined as what the customer demands. Based on statistical measuring tools, this discipline continuously seeks ways to improve the customer experience by reducing defects to the absolute minimum – the goal is zero.

Lean addresses efficiency, relentlessly eliminating waste using common sense methods in a well-organized and well-disciplined way. The real values of learning the Lean lexicon are to:
- Efficiently communicate with other team members to optimize production.
- Ensure every useful tool and technique is applied

Agile Development addresses timeliness, delivering significant efficiencies by speeding up the development process, ensuring the customer participates in developing what is wanted, and avoiding the wasted efforts of false starts and unnecessary work.

	Six Sigma	Lean	Agile
Characteristics requiring heavy use of tools of this discipline	Quantity production of precision items (including paperwork with high accuracy requirements)	Quantity production of anything	Regular introduction of new or revised products or processes
Some typical examples of elevated need	Aircraft, auto, machinery, equipment, banking transactions	Aircraft, auto, machinery, equipment, banking transactions	Computer hardware and software, kaizen business improvements
Some typical examples of more relaxed need	Gravel crushing, road building	Low-quantity production such as diamond cutting and artwork	Slowly evolving operations such as farming and steamship operations

This book also incorporates the seven classic visualization tools used to drive efficiency and effectiveness into production processes:

1. Ishikawa (cause-and-effect) diagram: used to logically connect issues to root causes
2. Check sheet: used to collect and organize information about production
3. Control chart: used to ensure production remains within specification limits
4. Histogram: used to understand performance variability by frequency of occurrence
5. Pareto chart: used to prioritize actions to correct problems by arraying them by frequency
6. Scatter diagram: used to correlate 2 variables from historic data to predict future outcomes
7. Flow chart: used to analyze a sequence of steps or events

These and many more appear in the chapter '*Applying the Tools to Get It Done*,' arranged in a logical sequence to identify and analyze problems, prioritize actions to fix them, identify obstacles, and organize a project to fix them.

The following 2 chapters describe in detail how to organize and run a kaizen event for rapid improvement, or a larger project for more complex improvements.

Because process mapping is particularly effective and can be complex, a chapter describes in detail the process for applying this tool.

The next chapter describes a method of identifying, evaluating and integrating the varied and often uncontrolled initiatives already in place in many or most organizations.

The final chapter addresses the problem of managing change in an organization of human individuals. In many organizations, change management is the most critical skill to master.

Introduction

NOTES:

_____

_____

_____

_____

_____

_____

_____

_____

_____

_____

Lean toward Lean

Lean Operations

An important recent framework for analysis and decision-making is that of a lean operation, focused simultaneously on:

<table>
<tr><td>

Elevator Pitch

"The 'Lean' philosophy focuses on the relentless elimination of waste based on a 'pull' production system."

</td></tr>
</table>

- Decreasing Waste, Cost and Cycle Time
- Increasing Capacity Potential
- Increasing Quality
- Low Absenteeism/voluntary Turnover
- Extensive Measurement of Key Processes
- High Levels of Worker Involvement, Ownership and Commitment

All of these benefits, and the ability to sustain them, are derived from the disciplined application of common sense tools and techniques that have been developed and refined in the manufacturing environment since the early 20th Century (see the chart on the next page for some of the heritage). For most traditional organizations lean requires a significant culture change, with executives and managers directly involved and floor personnel empower trained for continuous improvement.

Recently, the 'mass production' of transactions, documents, paper instruments, and records has created the need for lean operations in the clerical world ('Lean Office'), where higher quality translates into both operating efficiency and (often more importantly) improved effectiveness with highly leveraged benefits.

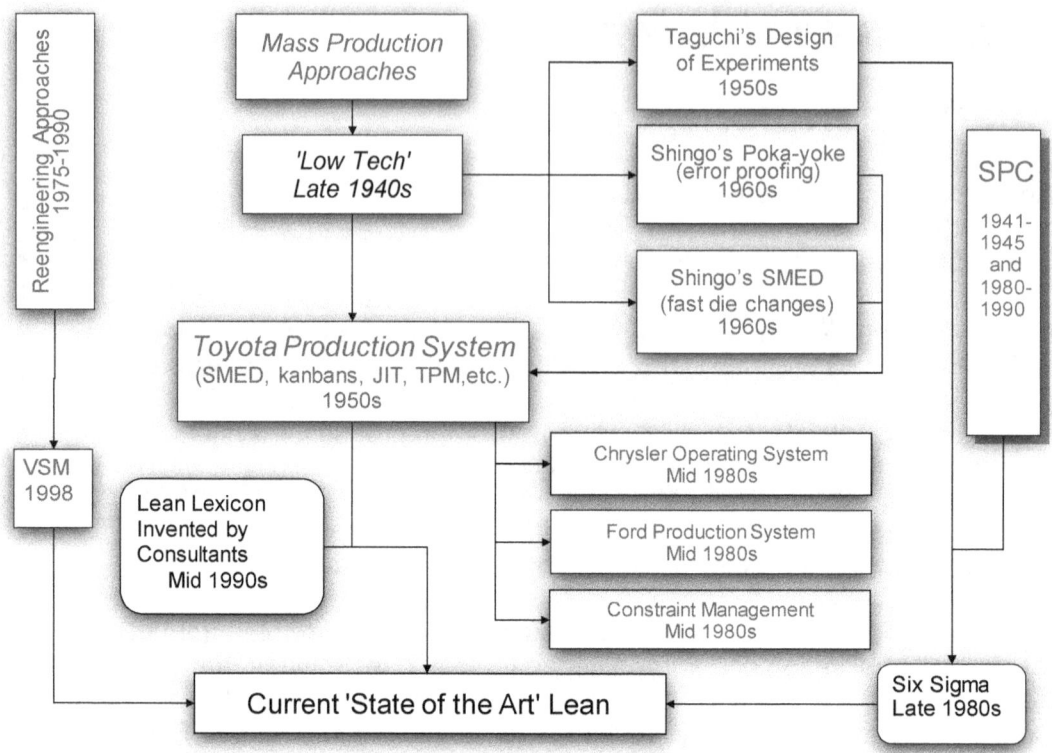

Why Lean is Important

Lean is the right approach to all repetitive activities in all organizations regardless of the goods or services they provide, because:

- Global competition is heating up as the Internet flattens the world
- Customers want fewer suppliers with better product quality and delivery reliability
- Customers want custom products at mass-produced prices
- Markets are price and value driven – costs are irrelevant to customers
- There is significant overcapacity in all significant markets
- Quality standards are very high, and rising, everywhere
- Technology is universal and does not offer anyone more than a temporary edge
- Investment money follows yields across industries – competition is unrelenting

Lean helps address these challenges by:

- o Designing capacity to meet demand, eliminating most excess capacity
- o Minimizing response time at the product, service and customer interface
- o Minimizing reaction time to problems
- o Minimizing assets (especially all types of inventory)
- o Minimizing delays (materials and products)
- o Maximizing flexibility
- o Maximizing throughput speed / minimizing throughput time

Resistance to Lean

Humans have never gravitated to organizing disciplines, and as work complexity increased in the industrial age the tendency has been to work in a rote manner based on engineering-type solutions with spurious precision. Few people really like to change, often through fear of wandering from the 'engineered' path into uncharted territory, and creating a lean team and a new culture often involves serious, fundamental change. When this is done poorly, failure to achieve lean reinforces existing weak practices and resistance to change increases.

Lean Tools and Concepts

Lean employs an impressive, sophisticated kit of concepts, tools and techniques, many of them complex enough to merit detailed explanation. This text deals with some of the key tools of lean in a sequence appropriate for a training class, beginning with foundational concepts.

Lean

Value Stream Mapping	
Area Display	TPM
Shift Huddles	SMED
	Constraint Management
Visual Workplace	
	Kanban
Poke-Yoka	One-by-One Production
5S	
Waste Identification	Pull System

In addition to these, lean employs tools shared with Six Sigma to identify, analyze, and correct processes that drive inefficiency, addressed in Chapter 4.

Lean Accounting

Lean Accounting focuses the business on the elimination of wasteful spending by aligning the financial measurement system with the value stream. Rather than continuously updating the costs of parts in WIP, this approach estimates the cost of finished products by combining all of the costs incurred in the value stream and dividing by the output for each accounting period. Since inventory is minimized and stabilized in the lean plant, the wasteful work of complex cost accounting is eliminated.

Often the first impact of lean accounting is DEGRADED cost performance, as excess inventories are eliminated and their costs are realized, but once in full effect the method frees up accountants to focus with lean teams on cost drivers that can be improved.

Elevator Pitch

"Standard cost accounting typically focuses on valuing inventory at all stages of production, and on keeping expensive machinery in production. Lean accounting instead focuses on value created in the overall value stream, and in optimizing the inventory even if key machines are occasionally idle."

Types of Waste ('Muda')

'Muda' (Japanese for 'waste') is everywhere. Since lean as a defined program started in the manufacturing environment (especially the Toyota Production System), many of the tools of lean refer to manufacturing type wastes. However, the principles apply equally well to the office, where 'production' might refer to a stream of transactions and 'inventory' might be a backlog of transactions. In the production facility, waste can mean the inefficiency of waiting for materials and the more expensive waste of producing out-of-spec product. Analogously, in the office, waiting for transactions is inefficient but doing them wrong can be disastrous.

Two other terms are used in the Toyota Production System to describe waste:

o 'Mura' (Japanese for 'unevenness') referring to disjointed production flow and addressed by Just-In—Time systems, line balancing, and kanbans

o 'Muri' (Japanese for 'by force') referring to the force-fitting of out-of-spec parts and addressed by standardized parts made with standardized processes

There are many types of waste to address. The chart on the next page illustrates a few 'usual suspects' to seek out in typical organizations. [1]

Production Waste

Source	How it Happens	Possible Root Causes
People & Equipment	Processing inefficiently	Process design, tools, skills, attitudes
	Excessive motion	Plant layout, moving devices
	Waiting	Process design, line imbalances
	Goal Alignment	Leadership, supervision
Quality	Scrap and rework	Processes, metrics, people
Inventory	Excessive Raw Materials	Supply chain issues
	Excessive WIP	Process design, poor or no kanbans
	Excessive Finished Goods	Marketing or transportation issues

Office Waste

Source	How it Happens	Possible Root Causes
People & Office Machines	Resources	Hiring, training
	Reporting	Organization structure, politics
	Processing inefficiently	Process design, tools, skills, attitudes
	Excessive motion	Workplace layout, moving devices
	Waiting	Process design, line imbalances
	Goal Alignment	Leadership, supervision
Team	Composition	Required skills availability
	Structure	Leadership, management
	Focus	Scope, culture, problem definition
	Conflict	Office politics, personalities
	Work Area	Size, layout, equipment
Process	Work boundaries	Roles & responsibilities, politics
	Sub-optimization	Process design, politics
	Lack of standardization	Process design, management
	Performance	Metrics, leadership
Tools & Technology	Capacity	Design, process evolution
	Integration	Cost, complexity
	Knowledge	Ease of use, skill requirements

Pull Philosophy

Elevator Pitch

"Pull systems attempt to produce goods only when needed and bring them to where they are needed."

The fundamental principle of lean production is a pull system. In a perfect pull system, nothing would be produced until it was demanded by a paying customer, in contrast to push systems in which products are pushed through manufacturing onto shelves where they wait for customers.

In that perfect pull system, a customer purchase would create a signal to the store, then to the warehouse, then to the manufacturer, then to the suppliers of parts, all the way back to the raw materials producers, and nobody would make anything until the customer acted. There would be no inventories of any kind except those actually being worked on or transported to the customer, and financial systems would not be designed to maximize machine utilization but to maximize the profit of the value chain.

Of course, there cannot be a perfect system. 'Monuments' – machines that touch every product – and other bottlenecks, along with unbalanced production capacity and physical distances to customers, require lead times for raw materials, parts, labor scheduling, and transportation, which in turn requires appropriate inventories along the value chain. These appropriate inventories are called 'kanbans,' described later.

Manufacturing Resource Planning (MRP) systems traditionally support push systems, attempting to place the right inventory in a factory in the right place at the right time to optimize production efficiency. While strong technology can also be used to support pull systems, attempting to ensure each station has just what it needs for production with no excess, a pull system is not dependent on technology for its success. It can be as low tech as a system of lights that are turned on or flags that go up when inventory reaches the prescribed kanban replenishment level, signaling for production at the next preceding stage. An effective pull system is primarily dependent on the people who operate it, using common sense and lean tools and techniques to continuously attack waste in the production process.

One by One Production

Elevator Pitch

"One by one production is an ideal seldom attainable. The practical goal is to reduce batch size to the minimum, trading off batch run efficiencies for minimum inventory."

In One by One Production (Single Piece Flow), products proceed one at a time through production. Ideally, there would be no interruptions, scrap or batch inventories anywhere on the line, and all materials would be work in process or finished goods on their way to a customer.

For example, in One by One Production, if a part moves through 3 one-minute steps it is ready after 3 minutes. In a batch of 100 pieces, it would have taken 300 minutes - 5 hours of inventory, and 5 hours any time the line needs to be restarted. Presumably the operators would stagger the batches to manage the work, but planning for this, and storing and moving the batches, will likely add work and space requirements that could be eliminated employing a batch size of one.

As a general rule, the smaller the batch size the better. However, optimization of batch sizes needs to consider the machinery and layout of the production area. Some inefficiency inherent in larger batch sizes might be offset by efficiencies in batch processing (e.g., equipment set up per unit may be reduced).

Chaku-Chaku

A 'chaku-chaku' line integrates humans and machines ('autonomation') to perform steps in a production process. The human operator loads the first machine, which automatically offloads to the next machine (using 'hanedashi' devices) when its production step is completed, and so on until human intervention is again needed; humans might be primarily overseers all the way to final assembly or shipping. By optimizing the machinery and its controls, the plant can approach a true one-by-one production system, with rapid adjustment of Takt time as demand changes, and quality may be better built into a line that minimizes human error.

Elevator Pitch

"Chaku-chaku is a production approach that automates a sequence of steps from machine to machine, minimizing the opportunity for human error."

If a chaku-chaku line begins to produce out-of-spec parts, operators are entrusted with the authority to stop the line instantly, and machines are designed to recognize abnormalities and automatically stop production as well ('jidoka').

Constraint Management

Elevator Pitch

"Every production line has a 'drum' – a process that constrains and sets the pace for the whole factory."

Every operation has a key constraint or bottleneck that limits output, thereby limiting the main goal of the operation (usually profitability in commercial enterprises). This constraint is a work process or key machine ('monument') through which every product must pass. The Theory of Constraints (TOC) aims to improve the flow (and throughput), pulling (rather than pushing) materials through the operation by focusing on the 'Drum,' the 'Buffer,' and the 'Rope' (DBR).[2]

The 'Drum' is the physical constraint of the plant, the work center or machine or operation that limits the ability of the entire operation to produce more. The rest of the plant follows the beat of the drum. Operators make sure the drum is always working and that the drum's output is fully utilized.

The 'Buffer' is inventory that protects the drum, so that it always has work flowing to it. Buffers are measured in time increments rather than quantity of material, setting priorities based on the time an order is expected to be at the 'Drum.' Buffers are maintained as raw or WIP inventory at the 'Drum' and at various synchronization points, and as finished goods ready for shipping.

The 'Rope' is the work release mechanism for the plant. An order is released into the plant only one 'buffer period' before It is due. Pulling work into the system earlier than a buffer time creates high work-in-process and slows down the entire system.

Eliminating the constraint at the 'Drum' moves the constraint to another part of the operation, which might be the next improvement target in a never-ending process. But this improvement process may require investments in labor or equipment, and must be weighed in light of the demand pulling product through the operation. The constraint will be irrelevant if there is insufficient demand to utilize the increased capacity. Business cases analyses may be required.

The Theory of Constraints considers four production flow designs to identify areas for improvement:

- I-Plant: Material flows in a sequence, such as in an assembly line. The primary work is done in a straight sequence of events. The constraint is the slowest operation.
- A-Plant: The general flow of material is many-to-one, such as in a plant where many sub-assemblies converge for a final assembly. The primary problem in A-plants is in synchronizing the converging lines so that each supplies the final assembly point at the right time.
- V-Plant: The general flow of material is one-to-many, such as a plant that takes one raw material and can make many final products. Classic examples are meat rendering plants or a steel manufacturer. The primary problem in V-plants is "stealing" where one operation (A) at a diverging point "steals" materials from the other (B). Once it has processed through A, it cannot come back and run through B without significant rework.
- T-Plant: The general flow is that of an I (or multiple lines), which then split into many assemblies. Most manufactured parts are used in multiple assemblies and nearly all assemblies use multiple parts. Customized devices, such as computers, are good examples. T-plants suffer from both synchronization problems of A-plants (parts aren't all available for an assembly) and the stealing problems of V-plants (one assembly steals parts that could have been used in another).

Step-by-Step [3]

1. Articulate the goal (e.g., "Make more money").
2. Identify the constraint (what prevents the organization from achieving the goal?)
3. Decide how to exploit the constraint (make sure the constraint is doing things that it uniquely does, and not doing things that it should not do)
4. Subordinate all other processes to above decision (align all other processes to the decision made above)
5. Elevate the constraint (if required, permanently increase capacity of the constraint; 'buy more')
6. If, as a result of these steps, the constraint has moved, return to Step 1. Don't let inertia become the constraint.

Throughput

Elevator Pitch

"Increasing throughput only helps if there is unmet demand, or if improved efficiency can be applied to reduce resources."

'Throughput' refers to the amount of product coming off the assembly line (or paperwork system). It can be increased by removing constraints, by applying more human or machine resources, or improved processes, methods, or procedures. Investments in removing constraints only help if there is demand for more product or if the constraint is causing inefficiency in the system, and measuring the benefits even then is a little complex. Before launching an effort to improve throughput, It is useful to understand the value, and the throughput / yield evaluation tool on the available CD can help.

Yield

The term 'yield' refers to the percentage of good product coming out of an operation compared to the input resources. An example is the manufacture of computer chips, where a large wafer with multiple chips is produced but some of the chips will not pass inspection and are scrapped. In a multi-step operation, the yield of each step factors into the final output. For example, if each of 5 steps yields 90% good product, the overall yield is .90 x .90 x .90 x .90 x .90, or about 59%.

Elevator Pitch

"Improving yield (good products per resources invested) gains more bang for the buck by definition. The only consideration is the investment required."

While improving throughput may not secure much benefit, depending on the demand drivers and operating inefficiencies, improving the yield of an operation is always a good way to reduce waste. But whereas lean tools generally apply more directly to the throughput problems, the sharp statistical tools of Six Sigma are generally required to improve yields.

Before launching an effort to improve yield It is useful to understand the value, and the throughput / yield evaluation tool on the available CD can help.

Focus on Reality

Elevator Pitch

"Problems are most effectively and efficiently eliminated by focusing the real work crew on the real parts in the real location using personally observed real facts."

The Toyota Production System espouses the philosophy that, in order to fix a problem, the people who are actually involved in the process creating the problem need to focus on the real products or parts that are being made ('gembutsu'), in the real part of the line where they are being made ('gemba'), based on the real facts of the situation ('genjitsu'), relying on personal observation ('genchi genbutsu').

In complex production processes, there is benefit in having industrial engineers design a production line and its steps. But to be lean, they must resolve problems and constraints with the real humans who will do the real work.

Visual Workplace

In the 'visual workplace' an uninstructed visitor can easily figure out what is happening. Floor traffic lanes are clearly marked, 'Area Goals & Metrics Boards' describe work area activities and performance, tool and part racks are color-coded, and prominent signs ensure safety and efficiency everywhere. It would take uncommon inattention to make errors.

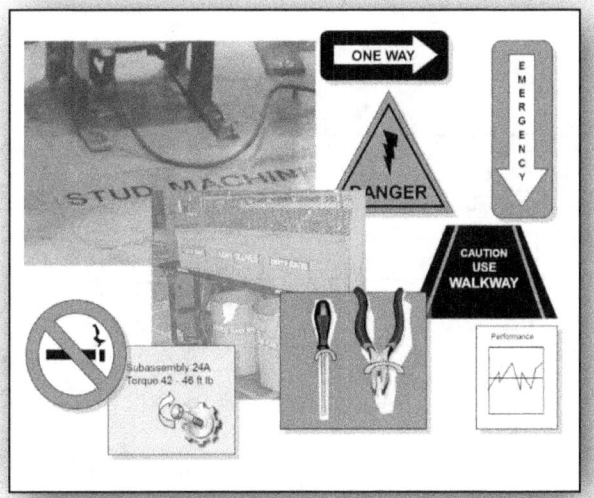

The visual workplace relies on excellent signage, with colors and icons that consistently reinforce common sense activities and material movements. Note the links to kanbans and the pull environment, where visual cues ensure that the correct material is called for in the correct quantity at the correct place. Lean production cannot be practiced effectively in a non-visual workplace.

Elevator Pitch

"Visual cues can make it dramatically easier for workers to maintain a safe, efficient workplace."

Step-by-Step

For each target process area:

1. Identify any worker issues that might arise from confusion, misplaced parts, etc.
2. Have informed visitors from a different department walk through the operation in question, taking notes on anything they don't understand
3. Assemble a team from the target area, plus others with visual workplace experience, if available
4. Use the issues and comments as a starting point and brainstorm what visual cues would contribute to safety, quality, and efficiency

Value Stream Maps

A fundamental insight of lean is that improvement efforts focus on each product and its value stream rather than the organization, its assets and technologies. A value stream map displays all of the steps required to deliver a product from raw material to customer delivery, and focuses especially on barriers to a smooth and timely flow.

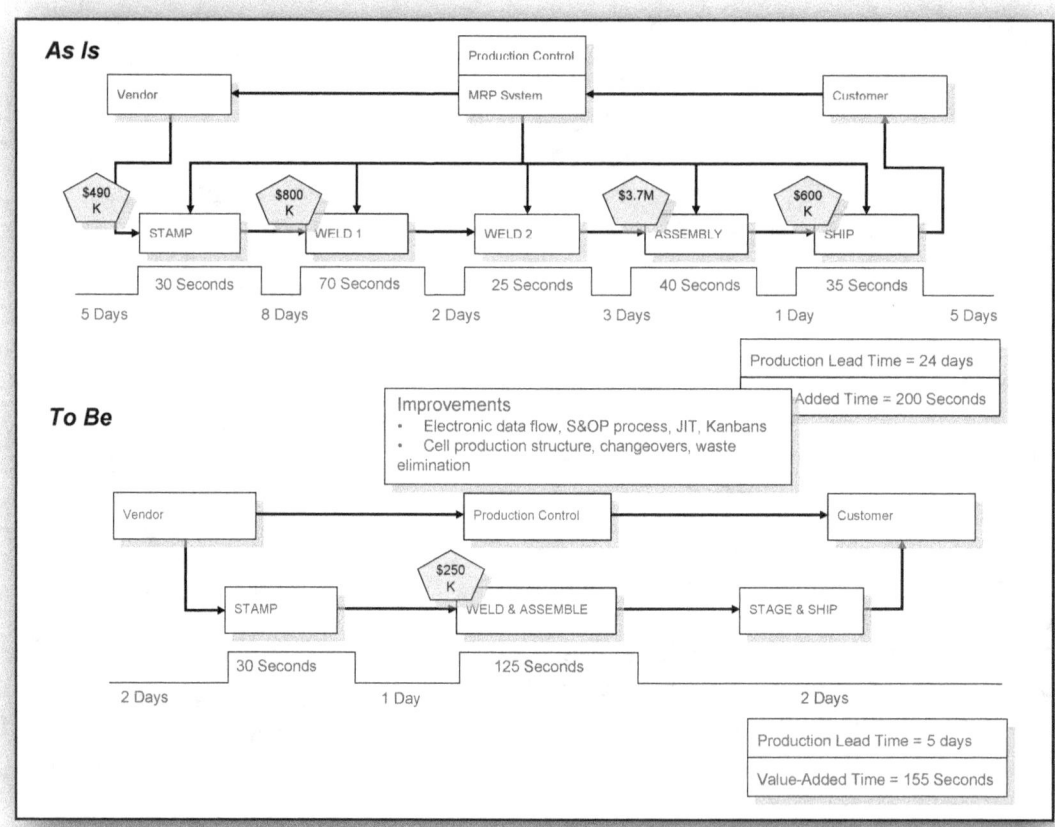

Step-by-Step

1. Assemble materials (such as a large inexpensive sheet of paper, tape, glue, markers, etc.)
2. Assemble a team that understands the processes
3. Define the scope
4. Define the process steps and sequence them on the paper from raw materials to finished products
5. Determine the actual process time for each step
6. Determine how much inventory exists at each step
7. Calculate 'turns' to determine how long inventory waits in each location
8. Review the map with the experts to identify improvement opportunities
9. Sketch out a possible 'to be' map with the experts
10. Iterate until a recommended map is generated

The total value stream might include a complex set of companies and plants, so It is useful to start with those activities bounded by the process owner ('door-to-door' within a plant, for example). This keeps the project at a manageable level of complexity but retains a sufficient 'big-picture' scope, required to avoid selective implementation resulting in isolated islands of improvement within a flawed process.

In the example shown on page 43, the 'As Is' and 'To Be' maps for a hypothetical organization are displayed to provide a sense of how improvements can be conceptualized. The wait and production times are captured at the bottom of each chart and inventories (in the shaded pentagons) are shown where they accrue, for easy visualization.

The value stream concept is of great interest to a process improvement team because it highlights wasted time, resources, and energy. It is also the starting point for defining a lean accounting system, helping the financial team simplify and significantly improve cost information. Lean accounting is beyond the scope of this chapter but information is available in the ROI-Team website library and from numerous other sources.

Line Balancing

Elevator Pitch

"A production line is balanced when each process step takes about the same amount of time, and less than Takt time."

Takt Time

  Total time available .
Required units produced

For example,

  480 min .   =   0.48 min
1,000 units

From the German word Taktzeit ("cycle time")

In a balanced production process, each step requires about as much time as other steps, as close to Takt time (the 'beat' at which finished units cross the finish line) as possible. For example, in building cars, 4 wheels need to be mounted at the same rate as 1 hood, 6 windows, 4 seats, and 1 steering wheel. Lean requires that steps in a production process be as balanced as possible, avoiding the wastes of inventory buildup, walking, and waiting.

Here, several of the production steps exceed Takt time, and none are perfectly aligned. Workers are walking and waiting at some stations while inventory piles up at others.

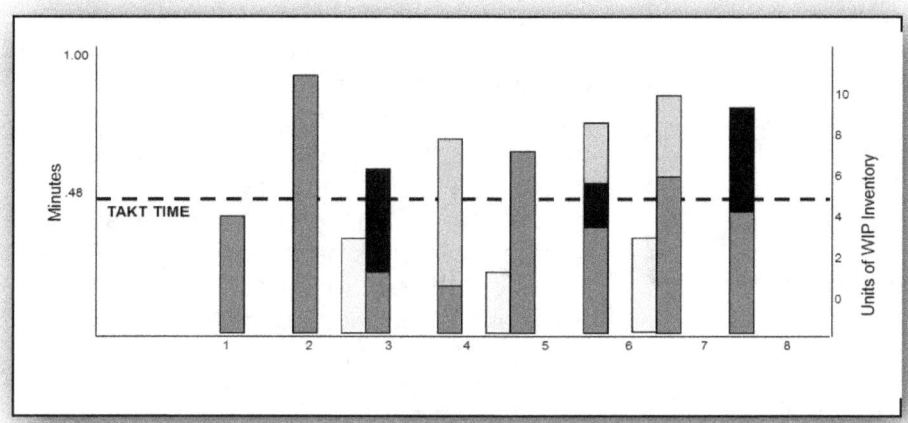

Some possible solutions to this imbalance include:

o   Work assignments: more workers might be required at station 2; stations 1 and 2 might be combined; and / or cross training might balance work among stations 2, 3 and 4.

o   Workplace layout (a 'spaghetti chart' would help in this analysis): station 4 might be moved closer to station 5; a conveyor might be installed; the productive work time might also be improved using better tool and part layouts in a more 'visual' environment.

The solution is dependent on the nature of each task and on the size and complexity of equipment, of course, and perfection is unlikely, but the work team can often improve such an out-of-balance condition using low-tech (and low-cost) solutions.

Standardized Work

Elevator Pitch

"Work standardization helps ensure processes (and results) are consistent."

Standardized work describes an individual worker's job as a series of defined steps, producing specific WIP quantities in as close to Takt time as possible. Its constraints are safety, quality and customer satisfaction, schedule, and cost. In lean operations, work stations are designed for efficiency and kanbans are defined to control the WIP movement; step-by-step standardized work becomes easy to define in this orderly environment. Here is a typical Standard Work Sheet, used to analyze a task or set of tasks.

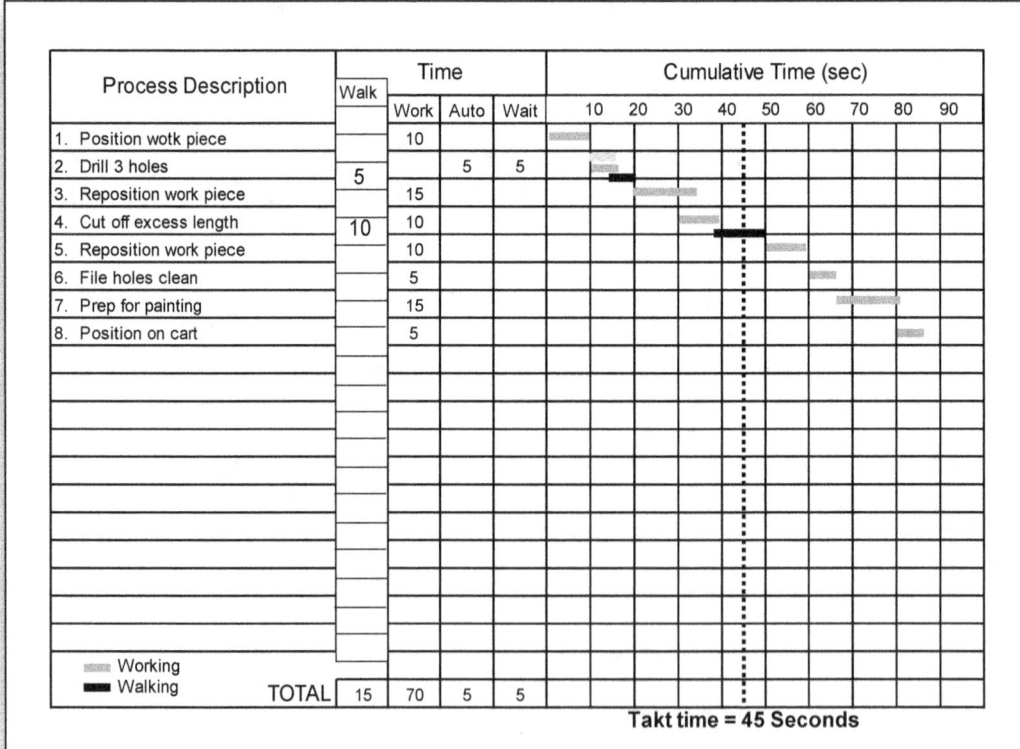

Process Description	Walk	Time			Cumulative Time (sec)								
		Work	Auto	Wait	10	20	30	40	50	60	70	80	90
1. Position wotk piece		10											
2. Drill 3 holes	5		5	5									
3. Reposition work piece		15											
4. Cut off excess length	10	10											
5. Reposition work piece		10											
6. File holes clean		5											
7. Prep for painting		15											
8. Position on cart		5											
▨▨ Working ▬ Walking TOTAL	15	70	5	5									

Takt time = 45 Seconds

In the example illustrated on page 48, the job requires more than Takt time. To resolve this, consider –

o   Could the work piece be positioned faster with better jigs and fixtures?
o   Could the equipment be positioned on the same table to reduce walk time?
o   Could the operator do something productive while holes are being drilled automatically?
o   Will additional workstations eventually be required to meet Takt time?

Step-by-Step

1. Define the starting and ending points (scope) of the task at hand
2. Establish exactly what happens to the work piece sequentially. This may be a challenge for the initial analysis, because different workers may do it differently (and the same person may do it differently from one time to the next)
3. Time each step: Because of variances in approach, times may vary radically. Develop a representative set of times, with worker involvement
4. Show the cumulative time graphically. Color code the work time, walk time, and automated time to facilitate analysis.
5. Analyze for opportunities

5S Principles

Elevator Pitch

"Lean production with Six Sigma quality is not possible in a disorganized, dirty workplace. In a lean audit, the 5S exercise is a very good starting point."

Step-by-Step

1. Use the checklist in this book or on the available CD-ROM (as is or adapted to your work environment) to create a 5S spider diagram for your organization.
2. On the checklist, enter the number 1 to 5 in the Rank column, to indicate
   1: Very Poor
   2: Poor
   3: Fair
   4: Good
   5: Outstanding
3. You can use or modify the audit checklist provided.

'5S' refers to the principle of waste elimination through workplace organization. The concept is derived from the Japanese words seiri, seiton, seiso, seiketsu, and shitsuke, with English counterparts:

1. Sort (separate needed tools, parts, and instruction from unneeded materials and to remove the latter)

2. Straighten or simplify (neatly arrange and identify parts and tools for ease of use)

3. Sweep or scrub (conduct a cleanup campaign)

4. Standardize (sort, simplify, and scrub at frequent intervals to maintain a workplace in perfect condition)

5. Self-discipline or sustain (form the habit of always following the first 4 'S' elements).

It is obvious that an orderly workplace is critical to lean operations, which rely on visual simplicity to keep parts flowing in response to pull signals. Safety is also improved in a clean and orderly environment, and an added benefit in many operations is that foreign matter is kept out of the products, with a direct quality impact.

The following chart shows the results of a typical 5S audit, using dummy data from the checklist on the next page. When all of these indicators fall in the 'good' or 'outstanding' blocks, workers spend very little time looking for things or working around spills and clutter.

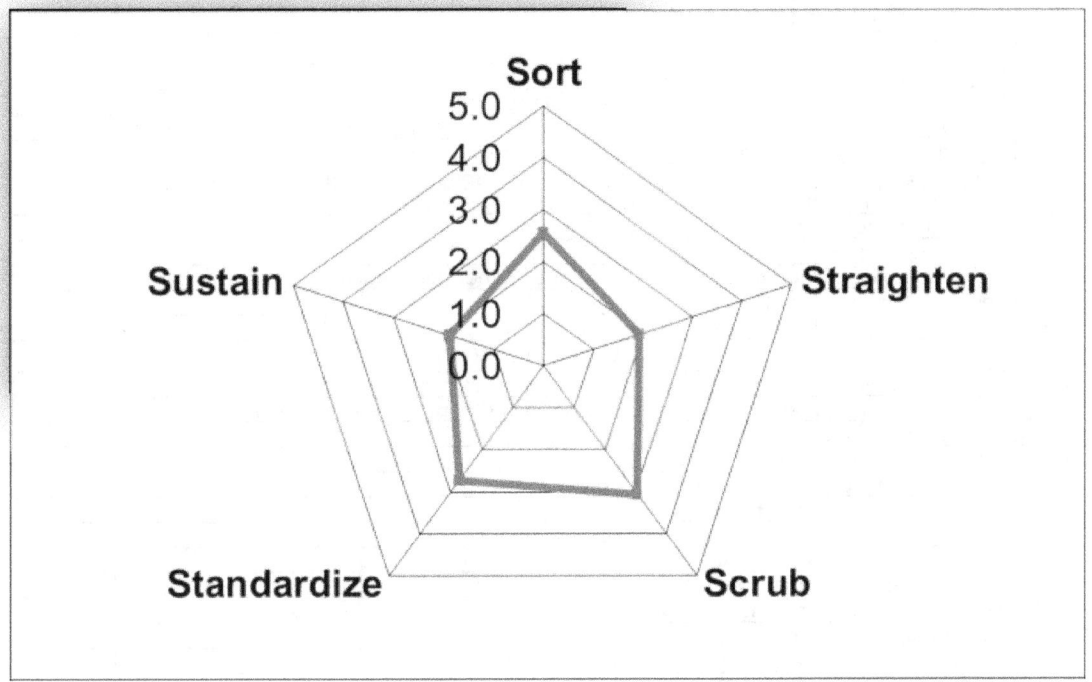

5S Audit Checklist

1. Sort	Rank
1 Inventory where it belongs	
2 Scrap / rework where it belongs	
3 Transit equipment well-maintained	
4 No unnecessary items / tools / paperwork in work area	
5 Posted notices appropriate and up-to-date	
6 Nothing on top of equipment or lockers	
7 Correct equipment labels	

2. Straighten	
1 Production flow direction and method well marked	
2 Aisles, power panels, and emergency equipment clear and accessible	
3 Equipment, tools, measuring devices, and supplies neat and convenient to operations	
4 Work area tools location identified, tracking system in place	
5 Pipes and wires in good repair, color coded with directions indicated as necessary	
6 Clear circuit diagrams / switch markings for electrical and fluid panels	
7 All items stored in work area clearly identified	
8 Moving equipment properly located	
9 Documents neatly stored in identified locations, ownership identified	
10 Desks neat and well organized	
11 Bulletin boards well maintained	

3. Scrub	
1 Wires and pipes connected neatly and safely to equipment	
2 Equipment, wires, and pipes protected and free of dirt, oil, rust, hydraulic fluid	
3 No equipment / pipe leaks	
4 Storage locations clean and orderly	
5 Power panels secured properly and safely	
6 Measurement equipment well cared for	
7 Gauges and indicator lights clean and easy to read	
8 Moving equipment well maintained	
9 Floor / aisles markings clear and intuitive	
10 Floors and walls clean and clear of dirt, oil, grease, hydraulic fluid, and trash	
11 Floor, wall, equipment, and pipe paint in good condition	
12 Benches and desks clean, orderly, and free of trash	

4. Standardize	
1 All hazards clearly identified	
2 Equipment controls clearly and correctly labelled	
3 Valves and switches clearly marked (on / off, open / shut, direction)	
4 Power / pressure meter ranges clearly marked	
5 Equipment status indicators in good working order	
6 Fan belts, chains, pulleys covered with size / capacity labels affixed	
7 Critical maintenance requirements and responsibilities clearly identified	
8 Equipment maintenance sheets current, clean, and neatly displayed	
9 5S status displayed and responsibilities identified and known by all workers	

5. Sustain	
1 Performance tracking visible and current - daily, weekly, monthly as appropriate	
2 Attendance and skills availability visible and current	
3 Continuous improvement / kaizen tracking visible and current	
4 Workgroup 5S audit score visible and current	

Total Productive Maintenance (TPM)

It is impossible to maintain an effective production schedule, and a lean operation, with random unscheduled interruptions. Total Productive Maintenance (TPM) is a disciplined approach to scheduled maintenance with an objective to gain optimum run time from every significant machine. Maintenance schedules are integrated with production schedules and rigorously enforced.

Preventive maintenance concepts (for example, knowing Mean Time to Failure (MTF) for significant machines, and planning maintenance accordingly), critical parts stocking, and shift maintenance resourcing are all keys to an effective TPM program.

One common approach is to schedule all planned maintenance off shift (in less than 24 hour operations) or during holidays or vacations. Others might feature investments in inventory build ahead or spare machines, parts, or assemblies. As in any equipment-dependent process, the quality of the maintenance team is key.

Elevator Pitch

"TPM (Total Productive Maintenance) merges the preventive maintenance schedule into the production schedule to minimize planned and unplanned down time."

Poka-Yoke

Elevator Pitch

"Poka-yoke is applied to methods, equipment, systems, and processes to make errors difficult or impossible to make. For example, stamping presses generally have safety gates and two-hand operating triggers to keep operators from reaching into a closing press."

Poka-yoke ('POH-kah YOH-keh') means 'fail-safing,' 'error-proofing,' or 'mistake-proofing,' and is a fundamental lean concept because it avoids two types of waste:

1. Repeatedly investing time in figuring out the right way to do something, And

2. Doing things erroneously, requiring rework or creating scrap.

The term means avoiding (yokeru) inadvertent errors (poka). It is a behavior-shaping constraint, or a method of preventing errors by putting limits on how an operation can be performed in order to force the correct completion of the operation. The concept was originated by Shigeo Shingo as part of the Toyota Production System. Originally described as Baka-yoke ('fool-proofing' or 'idiot proofing'), the name was changed to the milder Poka-yoke. One example is the inability to remove a car key from the ignition switch of an automobile if the automatic transmission is not first put in the 'Park' position, so that the driver cannot leave the car in an unsafe parking condition where the wheels are not locked against movement.

Shigeo Shingo recognizes three types of Poka-Yoke:

1. The contact method identifies defects by whether or not contact is established between the device and the product. Color detection and other product property techniques are considered extensions of this.
2. The fixed-value method determines whether a given number of movements have been made.
3. The motion-step method determines whether the prescribed steps or motions of the process have been followed.

Poka-yoke either give warnings or can prevent, or control, the wrong action. It is suggested that the choice between these two should be made based on the behaviors in the process, occasional errors may warrant warnings whereas frequent errors, or those impossible to correct, may warrant a control poka-yoke.

Elevator Pitch

"Kanban means 'storefront' and refers to the practice of treating production centers as standalone store-like demand centers, to pull inventory through a production process."

Step-by-Step

1. Kanbans are regularly updated as demand rises and falls
2. individual kanbans are calculated based on a number of factors, such as:
   o Flow rates set by throughput
   o Lot sizes upstream
   o Safety stock requirements
3. Visual signs are updated as kanbans are revised, and operators are informed

Kanbans

'Kanban' means 'store front' in Japanese, and refers to the shelf-stocking practices of supermarkets. In that pull environment, it is obvious when product supply is dwindling, and replenishment is automated according to rules that will maximize sales. In the manufacturing environment, the same principle can be applied, though it may require more inventory planning and supporting factory design to make replenishment points visually obvious.

Properly operated, the kanban system will tell much more than simply what amount of parts or subassemblies to stock. If stocks run out, the visual cues immediately highlight upstream problem areas. If stocks pile up, they highlight downstream problems. No data collection, analysis, or decision-making is needed to comprehend and focus on the problem.

Kanbans can be applied to work-in-process, buffer stocks, and transportation or warehouse stocks, following a few simple rules:

o Nothing moves without a kanban.
o Creation of kanbans is strictly controlled, usually by Production Control.
o The number of kanbans is strictly controlled, and continuously reduced.

Kanbans can be in bins, on trucks or forklifts or workbenches, or on a marked floor area, and need to be clearly identified for instant visual tracking.

The illustration here is of a typical identification system that marks a kanban area as well as racks of parts as they progress through an assembly operation.

Note how difficult it would be to computerize a kanban, continuously entering minute movements (including a few errors) and trying to follow part progress, compared to the straightforward visual system that kanban fosters.

Elevator Pitch

"SMED, or Single Minute Exchange of Die, refers to a disciplined approach to reducing machine setup time to the absolute minimum to support optimum operating flexibility and machine run time."

Step by Step

1. Record every step of the changeover process
2. Identify "Internal" and "External" steps
3. Reorder steps to ensure that no "External" actions are occurring while the machine is off
4. Create checklists and procedures to ensure everything is in place before the machine is turned off
5. Examine every "Internal" step for improvement
6. Observe and enhance operator effectiveness

Single Minute Exchange of Die (SMED)

Single Minute Exchange of Die (SMED) is a concept developed by Shigeo Shingo (of Poka-Yoke fame) to systematically reduce the changeover time (time to switch drills, cutters, dies, punches, and the like) required to set up equipment for production runs. The primary goal of SMED is to reduce lead time, for more agile market response and a host of related benefits. In addition, reduced set up times allow the reduction of batch sizes (see One-by-One Production) thereby reducing WIP inventories and associated inventory handling.

In reducing set up times, each step of the setup is identified as

o 'Internal' (the machine MUST be off during this step, as when parts are actually being removed) and

o 'External' (these should NEVER be done while the machine is off. For example, the setup person should not be looking for the new die while the machine sits idle).

'Internal' steps might be improved with machine modifications such as new fixtures or centering marks, or with visual workplace enhancements (tools well organized at the workplace, color-coded parts carts) and training. 'External' step improvements could include better material moving tools and techniques.

The illustration below shows how SMED supports a more efficient trade off of WIP carrying versus set up cost. Large lot sizes drive up the cost of carrying inventory linearly while the set up cost decreases, as depicted in the 'Before SMED' cost curve. Reducing the set up cost reduces the economic lot size, defined as the point at which total costs (inventory carrying plus set up) are minimized ('After SMED').

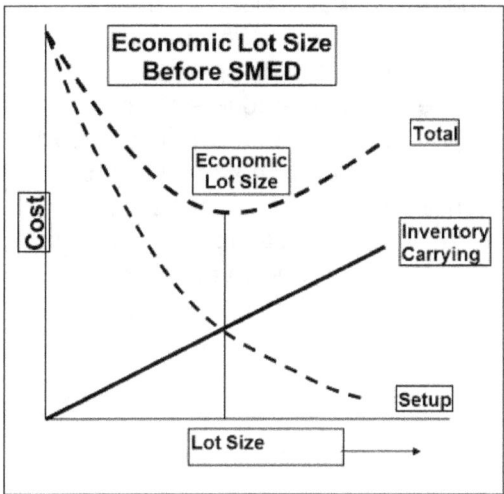 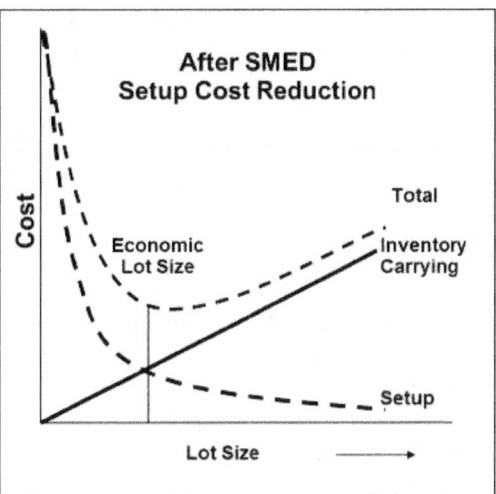

Spaghetti Diagram

Elevator Pitch

"A spaghetti diagram illustrates the actual physical flow of materials through a production process in order to design the most effective and efficient flow."

Step-by-Step

1. Get an accurate layout of the production area under study
2. Develop a sequential list of production process steps
3. Walk the floor from step to step and draw the flow on the layout
4. Take notes of area neatness, inventory, visual cues, and anything else impacting unobstructed flow
5. Analyze the flow for opportunities to eliminate travel distances and confusion

Workplace layout is a significant factor in creating a lean environment, directly driving motion waste and waiting time. If a work flow has evolved over time, it is likely that 'standard' work has evolved with it, incorporating significant material movement and wait time. The flow illustrated here is typical of that situation, with parts carried in, dropped off, moved around the stations, and eventually out the door. In this environment, it is easy to imagine rework parts mixed with good ones, time lost looking for parts, and numerous wasteful practices that keep the team busy but don't add value.

The 'spaghetti diagram,' named for the mess that too often exists, is a good place to start in developing the efficient standard work that lean requires. Once the diagram is drawn, improved flow patterns become intuitive, even when they involve immovable 'monuments.'

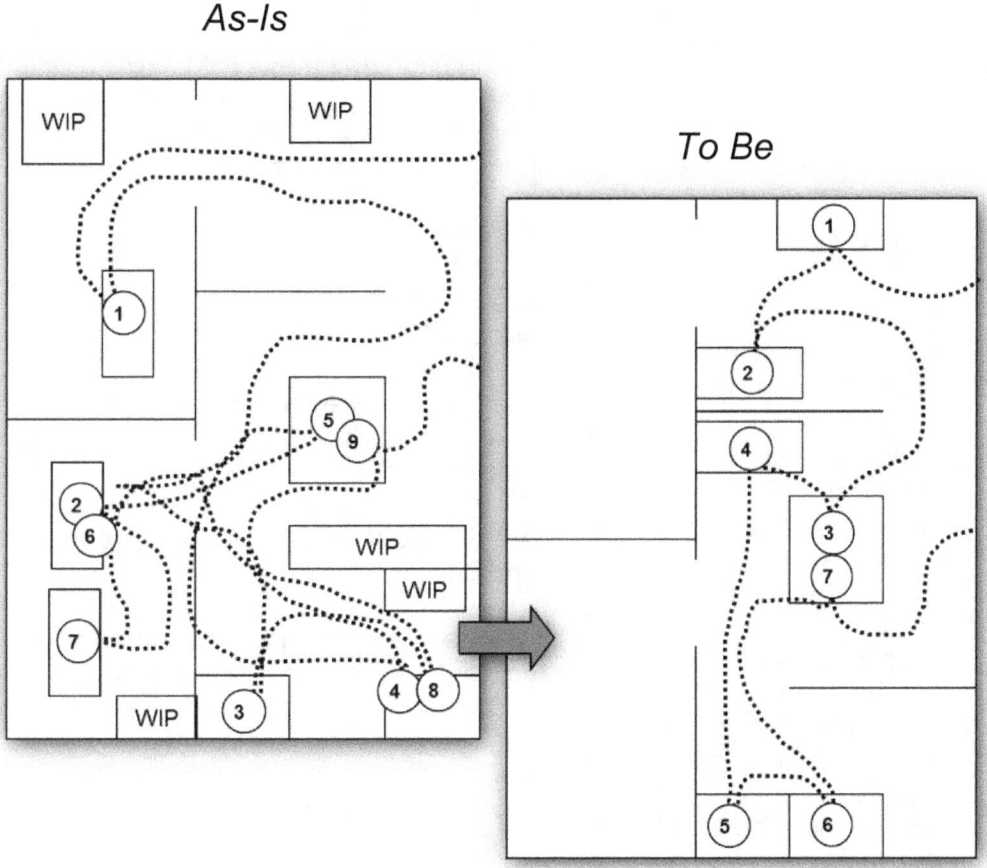

Ishikawa Diagram

Elevator Pitch

"An Ishikawa (or 'root cause') diagram logically connects a problem to its roots in an intuitive 'fish bone' format."

Step-by-Step

1. Correctly identify and define the problem
2. Assemble a team of experts (people who understand the problem) and brainstorm possible causes
3. For each cause, ask "why does that happen" and create sub-branches until the true roots are identified
4. As a team, develop a prioritized approach to solving the problem at its roots

The Ishikawa (or fish bone) cause and effect diagram is widely used to identify the roots of problems by successively asking 'why does this happen?' and drawing branches to represent the answer. The 5M approach illustrated here starts with the assumption that these 5 'M' factors include the 'usual suspects' in creating problems, and asks for each factor 'what prevents this from being wholly effective?'

For example,

Are people skilled, trained, and well-directed?

Are the machine capacities adequate to the requirements and are the machines well-maintained?

Are the methods standardized, controlled, and efficient?

Are the product's materials robust and appropriate, and are the suppliers reliable partners?

Are the right things being measured using capable instruments?

Ishikawa diagrams are often associated with Six Sigma problem solving, but this simple 5M approach is included in this discussion of lean because one or more of the 'M' factors can easily be overlooked.

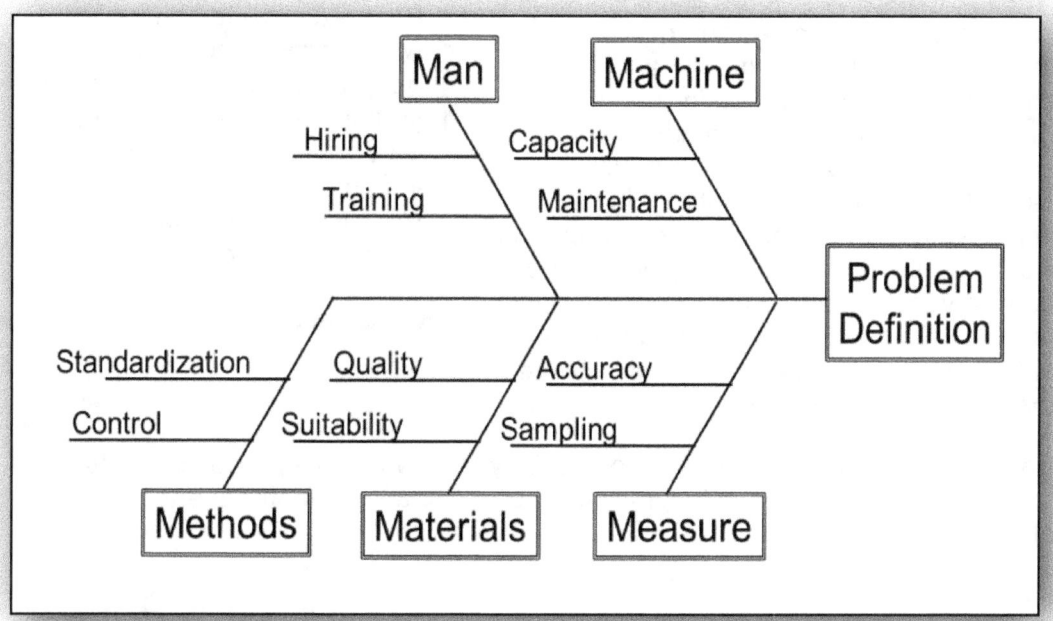

Insourcing and Outsourcing

In his excellent book "The World is Flat," Thomas Friedman notes that work of all types, and especially knowledge work, can be done anywhere on earth. In this world market what matters is quality and efficiency, and both are optimized in well-run organizations that have critical mass – sufficient sales volume to utilize their capacity and fund their continuous improvement programs. Insourcing (bringing work in-house that is currently performed by outside vendors) and outsourcing (finding reliable vendors to replace or supplement in-house capacity) are an important piece of the competitive equation.

> ### Elevator Pitch
>
> "In our flat world competitors win by producing quality goods efficiently anywhere. If you can make a purchased part better (quality and efficiency) insource it. If a reliable supplier has critical mass, outsource."

Each organization is challenged to regularly review its own production methods to determine, for every cost-significant product or service component of its offering:

If made in house:
o   Are we utilizing our dedicated resources at least 65%? (Less would suggest we might not be at critical mass.)
o   Does someone do it so much better that our cost would decrease if we bought outside? (Remember to factor in the cost of poor quality!)
o   Is this a critical core competence or scarce commodity that we can't afford to lose for its significant competitive advantage?

If Purchased:
o   Do we have underutilized resources that could be applied efficiently to this component?
o   Can we do it well enough that our cost would decrease if we made it inside?
o   Is this a critical core competence or scarce commodity that we need to better control for its significant competitive advantage?

The 'In-Outsource' Excel workbook on the available CD contains a robust tool for financial evaluation of insourcing or outsourcing work.

Daily Focus on Lean

Elevator Pitch

"Every work group needs a very brief stand-up huddle every day to ensure a coordinated effort. They also need an easy visual reference throughout the work day to stay focused on the critical objectives of the group."

Step-by-Step

1. Identify the target work group for a lean implementation
2. Have the affected managers and workers brainstorm the key elements of the group's mission
3. Translate those elements into a plan for information to display on the Area Goals and Metrics board, and to review in shift start up meetings
4. Continuously update and improve both the board and the meetings

Lean must become 'how business is done' in a work environment. This means there will be visual reminders everywhere, in the form of kanbans that force the right material to the right place at the right time, highly visible performance metrics that indicate how well customers are served, and highly visible tracking of continuous improvement efforts. Suggestion boards will place improvement ideas in front of the work team for immediate consideration and action. All of these cues are focused on the serious business of competing successfully with efficiently produced, high quality output. This information is organized for all-day reference on the Area Goals & Metrics board.

Another important lean element is the shift start up meeting (or huddle), which brings each working team together to focus on each day's work. This stand-up meeting (never exceeding 10 minutes) provides an opportunity to coordinate job coverage, problem awareness, production goals, and continuous improvement progress. A designated supervisor or team leader runs the meeting for every shift.

The shift start up meeting is held in front of the Area Goals & Metrics board, which is located in the immediate work area and updated each morning. This provides an agenda for the quick discussion.

In this example note the focus on the immediate work of the team. Since this is visible to the team throughout the work day, its message is never too far from consciousness.

A Typical Area Goals and Metrics Board

	Area Goals & Metrics for [Department Name / ID]
Team Photo	

Team
- Skills Matrix
- Scheduled Availability

Performance
- Key Metrics
- Performance Track

Current Issues
- White Board

Continuous Improvement
- Self Assessment
- Scheduled Projects / Progress
- Blank Suggestion Forms

Teams often assume initially that the Goals & Metrics board and shift start up meetings are 'Flavor of the Month' activities, and may erode the process by cutting corners, arriving late, or indicating that they don't take it seriously. This will eventually subside and the work teams will own the process if they see that management takes a genuine interest and that the process gains results. To ensure success, it is important to train teams well before they adopt lean disciplines, and to ensure that managers often attend the meetings and regularly participate in improvement events.

Uptime / Overall Equipment Effectiveness

Elevator Pitch

"OEE provides insights into the effectiveness of production equipment by measuring output versus capacity."

Calculations

o OEE: units produced as a % of capacity
o TEEP: units of output as a % of design capacity, in the total measured period (24/7)
o Loading: scheduled time as a % of total (24/7) time
o Availability: time actually available as a % of scheduled time
o Performance: actual output as a % of design capacity output for a period
o Quality: good product as a % of product started in the process

Overall Equipment Effectiveness (OEE) is a set of metrics that indicate how effectively a manufacturing operation is utilized relative to its design capacity. It is useful to consider OEE on a 24/7/365 basis (referred to as Total Effective Equipment Performance, or TEEP). Underlying this metric are several factors that help focus analysis teams:

o Loading, or scheduled operating time of the machine or plant
o Availability of the equipment (Uptime) considering planned and unplanned maintenance, for example
o Performance relative to design throughput
o First pass yield (quality of output)

OEE can be used to focus on a whole plant, a department, or a machine, in investigating problems with availability, performance, or quality.

Few if any operations run at 100% of capacity. Normal operations experience OEE in the 85% range.

NOTES:

_____

_____

_____

_____

_____

_____

_____

_____

_____

Agile Development

The Agile Development concept was initially applied to rapid, iterative, 'lightweight' software development, but many of the team and software structures fostered have been practiced in complex hardware development in a wide range of products: computers (like Dell), major aircraft, heavy equipment, automobile, and others who apply CADCAM, design-for-manufacturing, and simulation tools to dramatically cut development time and improve initial product performance.

Elevator Pitch

"Agile Development refers to rapid, iterative design of products enabled by small, independent teams with powerful software tools in order to rapidly respond to market opportunities."

Lean Production enables agile development by optimizing raw, in-process, and finished inventories in a pull system, minimizing obsolete inventories for better product life cycle management. Lean also places continuous focus on changing products and processes by stressing real-time shop floor communications using daily huddles, visual cues and information boards.

Consumers increasingly expect exactly what they want when they want it, and software tools have rapidly evolved to help create 'custom' products at mass-produced prices.

Agile Manifesto [5]

Issued in February 2001, this document states:

"We are uncovering better ways of developing software by doing it and helping others do it. Through this work we have come to value:
o   *Individuals and interactions over processes and tools*
o   *Working software over comprehensive documentation*
o   *Customer collaboration over contract negotiation*
o   *Responding to change over following a plan*
That is, while there is value in the items on the right, we value the items on the left more."

NOTES:

Achieve Six Sigma Quality

Introduction

W. Edward Deming was the production statistician who developed the quantitative tools and techniques that reset quality expectations across industries worldwide. After established U.S. and European industries rejected his statistical process methods in the 1950's, Japanese manufacturers adopted his concepts and captured a significant share of world markets in automobiles, electronics, and other consumer goods before other regional markets could react. Following the Japanese lead, many consulting organizations, internal and external, have developed tool kits for continuously improving business processes.

Elevator Pitch

"Six Sigma refers to the sixth standard deviation from the mean of a normal curve, applied to production to mean about 3.4 errors per million parts produced – very high quality indeed. The term has also been extended in popular usage to refer to a program with a defined tool kit designed to produce Six Sigma quality."

W. Edward Deming [6]

With a major commitment to defense against foreign competition in the early 1980's, Motorola developed particularly successful practices to systematically improve processes by eliminating defects, and trademarked the term 'Six Sigma' to refer to its system. General Electric's implementation of 'Six Sigma' features definable, repeatable processes executed by dedicated professional 'green belts' and 'black belts.'

Mathematically, 'Six Sigma' refers to six standard deviations from the mean of a normal curve (a mathematical tool for analyzing variances). A process that achieves or exceeds a Six Sigma level of quality will by definition have 3.4 errors, or fewer, per million. Like lean production in the prior chapter, Six Sigma is a philosophy, in this case dedicated to delivering consistently the quality customers demand.

Some organizations have attempted to apply the Six Sigma concepts and toolkit to activities with relatively low throughput or non-repetitive tasks. In such cases it is better, when errors are unacceptably expensive, to use the error-proofing tools of lean rather than the process control tools of Six Sigma.

This chapter reviews the basic concepts and tools of the most effective quality programs.

Total Quality Management (TQM)

Total Quality Management (TQM) is a widely used strategy aimed at embedding quality awareness in processes throughout an organization, to improve effectiveness and efficiency while increasing customer satisfaction.

Quality assurance through statistical methods is a key component of TQM, starting with testing random samples of product for qualities demanded by customers. Root causes of any failures are identified, analyzed, and corrected. Statistical Process Control charts track production quality in real time, and when measures drift out of limits the process is fixed. The upper and lower control limits are set tighter than levels where the product would fail, ensuring the process will be fixed before failing products are produced.

Elevator Pitch

"TQM – Total Quality Management – applies statistical methods to ensure quality standards are met wherever products are made, throughout an organization."

"Quality is Free" [7]

In his highly regarded book, Phil Crosby espoused "Doing it Right the First Time (DIRFT) and outlined these 4 key concepts:

1. *The definition of quality is conformance to requirements*
2. *The system of quality is prevention*
3. *The performance standard is zero defects*
4. *The measurement of quality is the price of nonconformance*

ISO 9000

> ### Elevator Pitch
>
> "The International Standards organization has created a number of ISO standards for how a company should operate to create products of consistent quality. These standards have been widely accepted, and ISO 9000 certification is important for marketing across a broad spectrum of complex products."

ISO 9000 is a family of standards for quality management systems. ISO 9000 is maintained by ISO, the International Organization for Standardization and is administered by accreditation and certification bodies. For a manufacturer, some of the requirements in ISO 9001 (which is one of the standards in the ISO 9000 family) would include:

o A set of procedures that cover all key processes in the business
o Monitoring manufacturing processes to ensure they are producing quality product
o Keeping proper records
o Checking outgoing product for defects, with appropriate corrective action where necessary
o Regularly reviewing individual processes and the quality system itself for effectiveness

A company or organization that has been independently audited and certified to be in conformance with ISO 9001 may publicly state that it is 'ISO 9001 certified' or 'ISO 9001 registered.' Certification to an ISO 9000 standard does not guarantee the compliance (and therefore the quality) of end products and services; rather, it certifies that consistent business processes are being applied.

Although the standards originated in manufacturing, they are now employed across a wide range of other types of organizations, including colleges and universities. A 'product', in ISO vocabulary, can mean a physical object, or a service, or software.

Baldrige Award

The Baldrige Award is given by the President of the United States to businesses—manufacturing and service, small and large—and to education, health care and nonprofit organizations that apply and are judged to be outstanding in seven areas: leadership; strategic planning; customer and market focus; measurement, analysis, and knowledge management; human resource focus; process management; and results.

> ## Elevator Pitch
>
> "The Baldrige Award was created to recognize organizations with quality and performance excellence that added to America's competitiveness in an increasingly competitive world market."

Congress established the award program in 1987 to recognize U.S. organizations for their achievements in quality and performance and to raise awareness about the importance of quality and performance excellence as a competitive edge. The award is not given for specific products or services. Three awards may be given annually in each of these categories: manufacturing, service, small business, education, health care and nonprofit.

While the Baldrige Award and the Baldrige recipients are the very visible centerpiece of the U.S. quality movement, a broader national quality program has evolved around the award and its criteria. A report, Building on Baldrige: American Quality for the 21st Century, by the private Council on Competitiveness, said, "More than any other program, the Baldrige Quality Award is responsible for making quality a national priority and disseminating best practices across the United States."

The U.S. Commerce Department's National Institute of Standards and Technology (NIST) manages the Baldrige National Quality Program in close cooperation with the private sector.

Normal Distribution (Bell Curve)

Elevator Pitch

"The Bell Curve is a foundational concept of statistics, applicable to a broad range of natural phenomena. It demonstrates that the frequency of any measurement decreases predictably as the distance from the mean increases."

The normal distribution, also called the Gaussian distribution, is an important family of continuous probability distributions, applicable in many fields. It is often called the bell curve because the graph of its probability density resembles a bell. The central point on the curve represents the mean ('average', μ) and variance from this point is known as standard deviation, usually denoted by the Greek symbol Sigma (σ). The standard normal distribution is the normal distribution with a mean of zero and a variance of one.

The mean is easy to derive, calculated as the sum of the measurement of all units in the sample divided by the number of units One sigma is calculated as the square root of the sum of the deviations squared divided by the number of units in the population (formula shown), while the shape of the curve requires more complex mathematics.

Sigma calculations indicate that 68.27% of the population will fall within one standard deviation above or below the mean, 95.45% within two, 99.73% within three, and increasingly higher percentages with each sigma step thereafter.

Six Sigma is defined in business improvement programs as 3.4 defects per million (the inverse of 99.9999966% falling within the acceptable range), though this is nominal, not a precise statistical calculation.

An example of a Bell Curve appears on page 75.

A simple illustration of normal distribution is the height of adult humans. There is an average height, and variances from this average (taller or shorter) become statistically rarer as the variance increases. Whereas hundreds of millions fall within a few inches, it is very rare to find a person 2 feet taller or shorter.

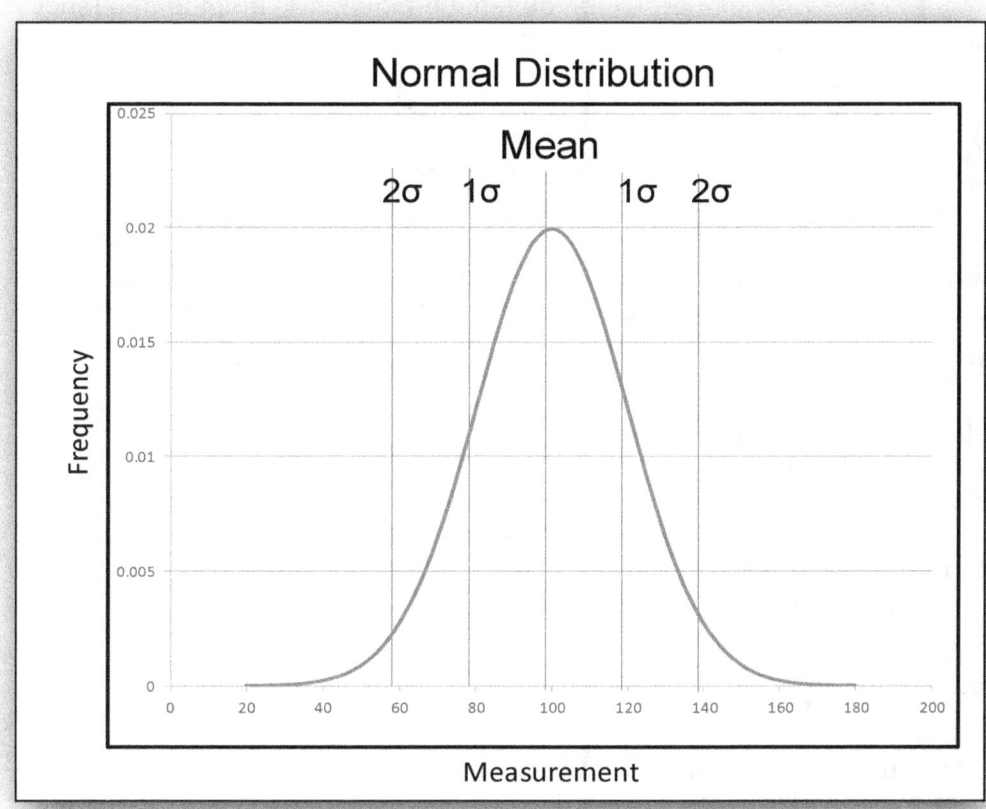

Histograms

Elevator Pitch

"Histograms depict the frequency of measurements along a continuum. A very large sample takes on the characteristics of a Bell Curve."

Histograms are graphic representations of how often something occurs. The metric appears on the x axis and the frequency on the y axis.

For a critical product specification, this quality tool will help the production team ensure compliance with the spec using SPC techniques described on page 78. The example illustrated (page 77) shows how often an I-Beam is produced longer or shorter than its standard length.

Step-by-Step

Refer to the illustration on page 77. In designing a histogram, consider:

1. How many data points will be collected (here, several hundred)
2. What the range will be (I-Beams 11' 11 1/10" to 12' 1/10")
3. How many classes of data (generally 7 – 10, maximum 20 – 30)
4. What data ranges will be represented on the chart (21, each 1/100th of an inch, centered on the standard length)

In this example, the histogram more nearly approximates a typical bell curve as data points are added, and production of the I-Beams appears to be controlled. If there were production problems, the curve would tend toward irregularity such as bi-modality (more than one process at work) or skewing (unbalanced control tendencies).

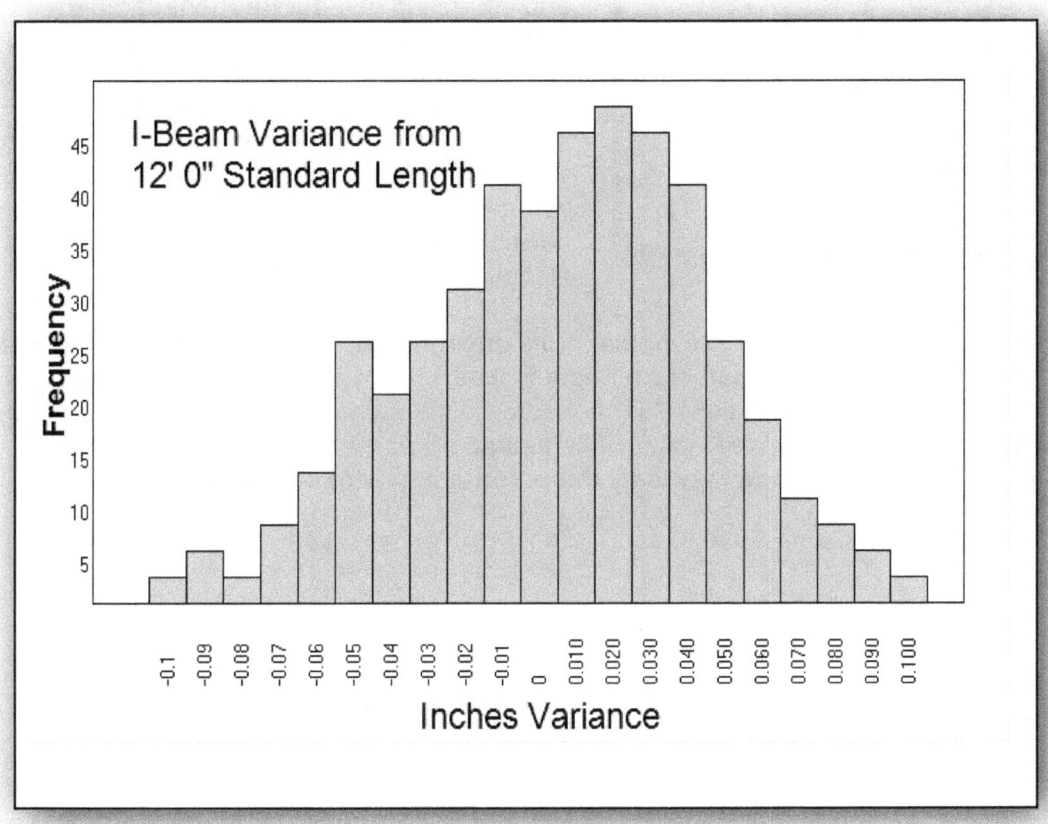

Statistical Process Control (SPC)

Elevator Pitch

"Statistical Process Control (SPC) charts track key metrics in production to provide early warning when processes begin making out-of-spec products."

Statistical process control (SPC) is a method of visually monitoring production processes. With the use of control charts and collecting few but frequent samples, SPC can effectively detect changes in a process that may affect product quality. There is variability in any production process, and product properties usually vary slightly from their designed values even when the production line is running normally. These variances can be analyzed statistically to control the process.

If the production process, its inputs, or its environment changes (for example, the machines doing the manufacture begin to wear) this distribution can change. Process performance is typically tracked on control charts like the one illustrated, which record specified metrics for each sampled part and provide an intuitive visual impression of how precisely the process is controlling output.

In the example illustrated, a plastic parts line may be designed to create parts weighing 1.75 kg, but some parts will weigh more than the target and some will weigh less, in accordance with an expected distribution. In this illustration, It is acceptable for the plastic part to weigh .05 kg more or less than the target, and in the first part of the chart random fluctuations indicate that it is performing acceptably. But in the middle of the chart, non-random fluctuations warn the team to determine the root cause and take corrective action. In this example, perhaps the injection screw pressure is too high, causing the molding machine to put more plastic into each part than specified. If this change is allowed to continue unchecked, more and more product will be produced that falls outside the tolerances of the manufacturer or consumer, resulting in waste, in this case excess material cost or even rework or scrap.

Statistical Process Control Example

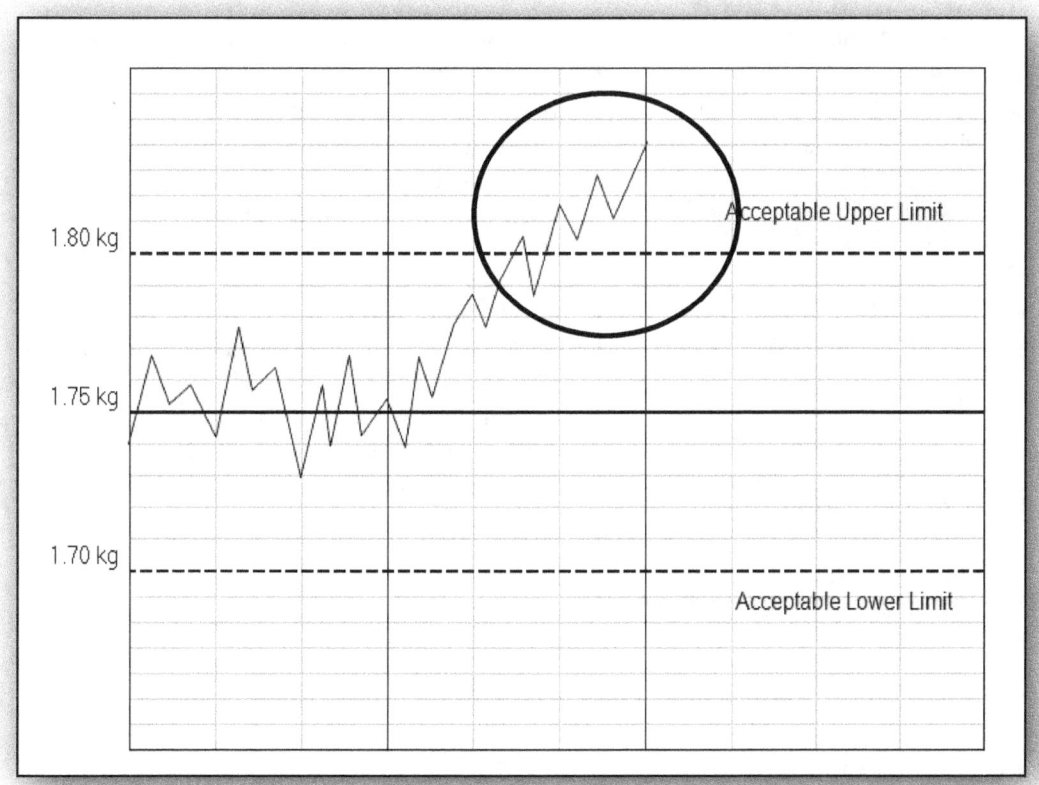

XbarR Charts

Elevator Pitch

"XBar charts track multiple samples in production to help determine whether errors are due to random events or to special causes that can be corrected."

Step-by-Step

1. Collect samples per a plan developed by statisticians
2. Create the XBar chart and the Range chart, as illustrated
3. On the Range chart, look for out-of-control points.
4. After reviewing the Range chart, look for out-of-control points on the X-bar Chart.
5. If there are any, brainstorm and conduct Designed Experiments to find and correct the root causes.

An XbarR chart is a member of a family of control charts, tools used in quality control (SPC) as originally developed by Walter A. Shewhart at Western Electric in 1924 to improve the quality of telephones. The purpose of any control chart is to help determine if variations in measurements of a product are caused by small, normal variations that cannot be acted upon, or by some larger special cause that can be fixed. The type of chart to be used is based on the nature of the data.

An XbarR chart is used when you can collect measurements in groups of ten or fewer observations. Each group represents a snapshot of the process at a given point in time (on the x axis), collectively showing a history of process performance in terms of Xbar (the mean measurement of the attribute being tracked) and Range (the variation of the observations within the group).

Each chart centerline represents the mean of all groups, the upper dashed line is the upper control limit or UCL and lower dashed line is the lower control limit or LCL, plus and minus three standard deviations from the overall average respectively.

In this example, the data in the top chart might represent the lengths in inches of I-Beams produced, and group 1 (the first point) might have values of 69, 73, 76, 71, and 70, with a mean of 71.8, calculated as (69 + 73 + 76 + 71 + 70) / 5.

The bottom chart has the range (R) of each subgroup plotted in a similar manner. In the case illustrated, the range for group 1 is 76 (the longest) minus 69 (the shortest) or 7 inches.

Calculations of means, ranges, and standard deviations use straightforward statistical methods found in many statistics textbooks.

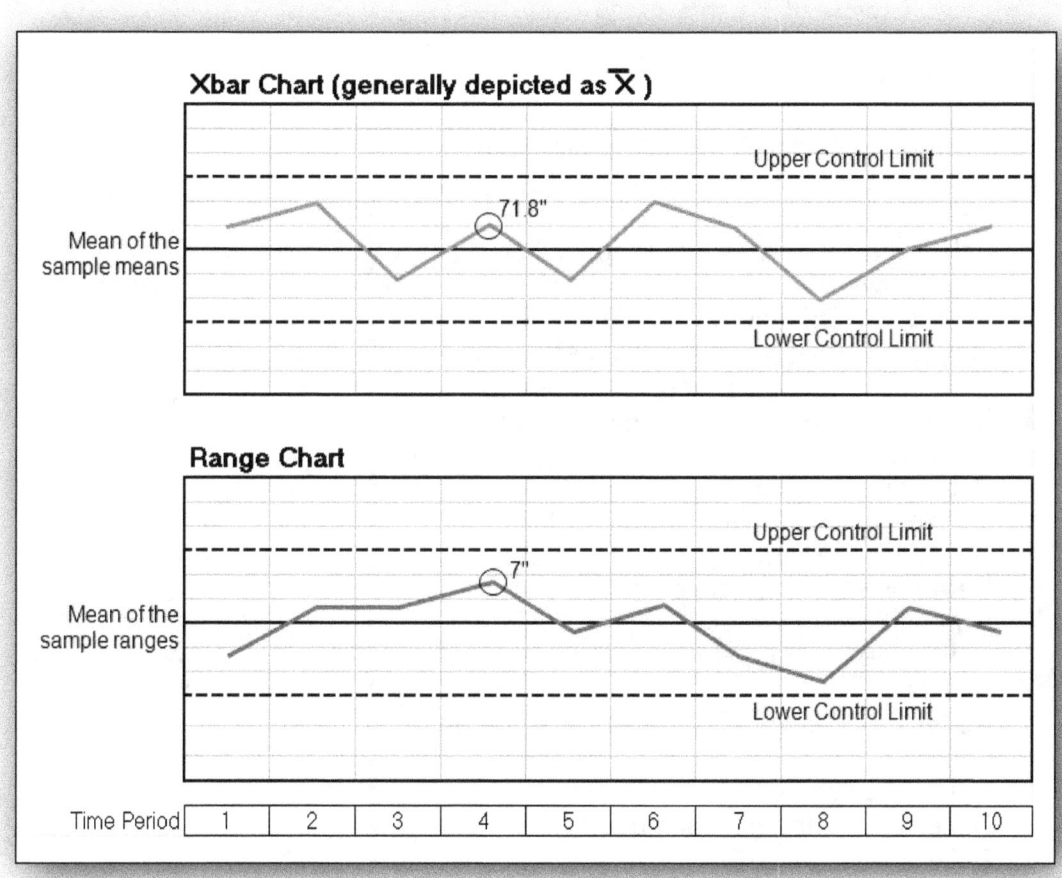

Design of Experiments (DOE)

Elevator Pitch

"Design of Experiments brings a method of disciplined observation to solving process problems."

Design of experiments (DOE) is the design of manipulation, observation and analysis procedures where variation (in product quality, for example) is present to determine the causes of variation. The concept has a broad application across all the natural and social sciences, and can be applied productively to business applications.

Step-by-Step

DOE is methodical, typically following these steps:

1. Select the problem (Who, What, When, Why, How)
2. Determine dependent variables to be measured using performance measures, subjective measures, or physical responses
3. Determine independent variables to be manipulated
4. Determine the number of levels of independent variables (number of conditions to be manipulated)
5. Determine the possible combinations of independent variables
6. Determine the number of observations required
7. Redesign (if flaws or inconsistencies crop up)
8. Randomize research participants
9. Develop a mathematical model
10. Collect data
11. Rationalize and analyze the data to understand the drivers of variance
12. Verify the data

Taguchi (DOE)

Statistical methods developed by Genichi Taguchi to improve the quality of manufactured goods center on zeroing in rapidly on the variations in a product that distinguish the bad parts from the good. The point is to avoid endlessly testing for all the possible defects. Taguchi Innovations in the design of experiments are considered controversial among some traditional Western statisticians but others accept many of his concepts as being useful additions to the body of knowledge.

Taguchi's principal contributions to statistics are:

o   Loss-function: quality engineering should start with an understanding of the cost of poor quality, including costs to society
o   The philosophy of off-line quality control: the best opportunity to eliminate variation is during design of a product and its manufacturing process

Shainin (DOE)

Solving chronic quality issues has been an increasing challenge for many decades, with increasing technology complexity, narrower specification ranges, and the many factors and parameters involved making it ever more difficult to identify root causes. To address this challenge, Dorian Shainin, an influential American quality consultant, developed Design of Experiments (DOE) statistical techniques that have the advantage of being simple but powerful and widely applicable for finding the most important root causes of variation (Shainin's 'Red X') following the Pareto '80-20' rule. Shainin's DOE has a reputation for solving real life complicated quality issues and is considered a significant breakthrough in quality analysis.

Elevator Pitch

"QFD is a tool used by a cross-functional team to address and coordinate product development to ensure right-first-time performance and on-going success."

Step-by-Step

1. ID customer needs, prioritized
2. Analyze competitive opportunities (Us vs. Competitors, scale of 1 to 5 illustrated, could be a useful approach)
3. Set target values for critical success criteria and plan a product for the opportunity (using characteristics such as those shown in the first row)
4. ID Critical Parts/Services and set target values for critical parts/services characteristics
5. ID critical processes and set critical process ranges/KPIs
6. Develop process equipment to meet targets

Quality Function Deployment (QFD)

Quality function deployment (QFD) is a comprehensive group decision making tool used in product or service development and product management. QFD focuses cross-functional teams on key trade-offs to achieve performance targets for new or existing products or services, from the viewpoints of market demands, company goals, and technology realities. The use of QFD eliminates expensive rework as projects near launch. QFD is applied in a wide variety of products and services and is considered a key practice of Design for Six Sigma (DFSS).

Typical QFD development starts with the voice of the customer and considers the products needed, the critical components that go into those products, and the processes needed to produce the products effectively (right quality) and efficiently (right cost), prioritizing characteristics and setting development targets. The team can also consider technical capabilities versus those of competitors, and the degree of technical challenge, to ensure the deck is stacked for success.

QFD House of Quality

The QFD example illustrated below suggests how the interaction of demands and capabilities is depicted to highlight priorities and tradeoffs.

Quality Function Deployment Example

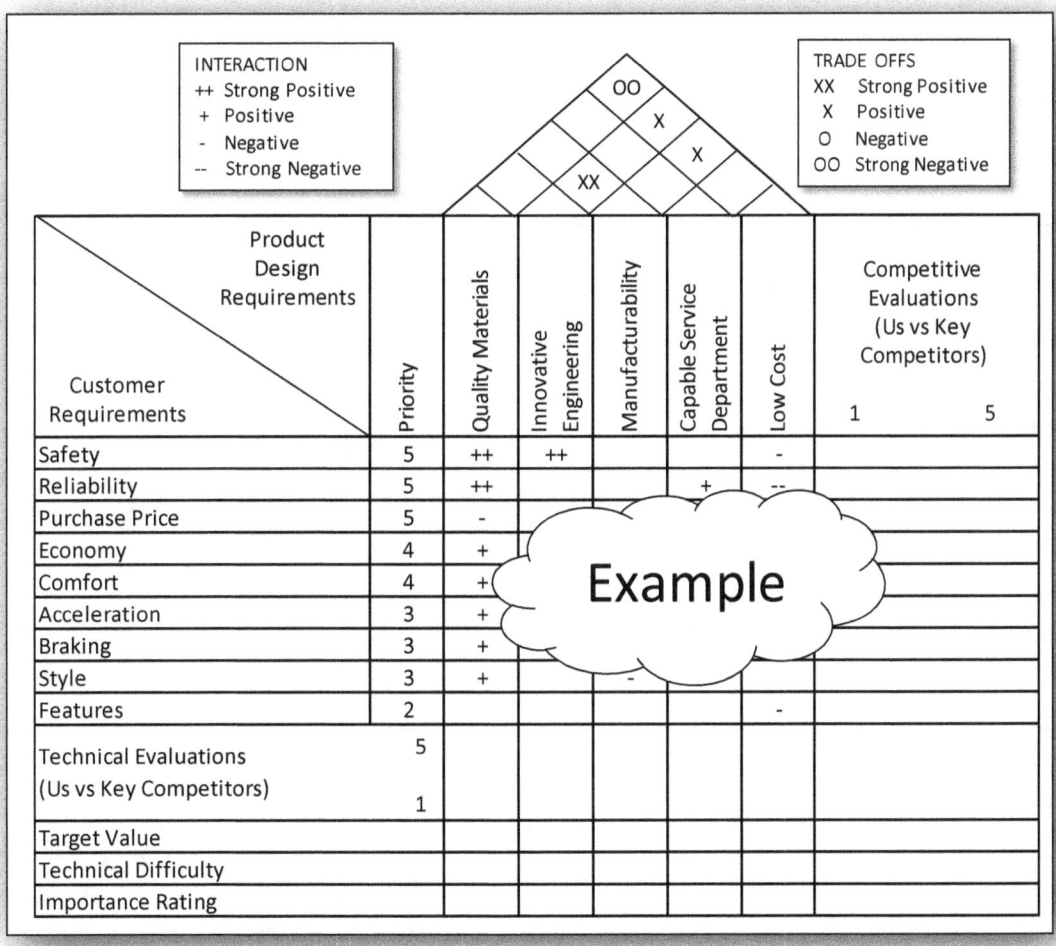

NOTES:

Apply the Tools to Get It Done

Tool Application Sequence

The tools used to correct efficiency problems (lean elimination of waste) and to correct effectiveness problems (Six Sigma production of products that meet customer requirements) are essentially the same, and require the same planning, teamwork and executive sponsorship to succeed.

Regardless of which type of problem is being addressed, the tools are used in a logical sequence to identify and analyze the problem, prioritize the fixes, estimate the challenge, and establish a project.

> **Elevator Pitch**
>
> "Lean and Six Sigma tools are the same, and require the same planning, teamwork, and sponsorship."

Purpose	Tools
Identify the Problem	Brainstorming, Process Flow Analysis, Day in the Life Of (DILO) Studies, Ratio Delay Analysis
Analyze the Problem	Check sheet, Scatter diagram, Ishikawa Diagram, Affinity Diagram
Prioritize Actions to Fix the Problem	Pareto Analysis, Failure Modes and Effects Analysis (FMEA), Multivoting
Estimate the Challenge	SIPOC, Force Field Analysis
Establish a Project	Generic Process, DMAIC, Design for Six Sigma (DMADV of DFSS)

Brainstorming

Elevator Pitch

"Brainstorming is a simple and effective way to quickly get an appropriate set of ideas about any subject. In operations analysis it is particularly effective in defining problems and hypothecating solutions."

Step-by-Step

1. Assemble the right team of experts
2. Correctly identify the problem to be solved
3. Generate ideas: post the rules of the road on the wall for reference. No idea is a bad idea while the team is freewheeling
4. Clarify the ideas: ensure the team has a common understanding of each item, and group duplicates or restatements of the same idea
5. Evaluate: discuss and prioritize or eliminate ideas to develop the best approaches

Brainstorming is used any time there is value in getting everybody's input on the table. The concept of brainstorming is intuitive, but it helps to apply it systematically, and to ensure the team understands the rules, especially:

1. Get as many ideas as possible
2. There are no silly or bad ideas
3. Everyone joins in
4. Hitchhiking (building on another's ideas) is okay
5. There are no judgments or discussions of ideas while ideas are being generated

Focus Groups

Focus Groups are organized to provide insights from about 6 to 12 individuals with points of view on a particular set of questions. For example, they are often used by product designers to try out concepts such as product look and feel, features, and the like, and are generally made up of potential users of the product. A focus group meeting is analogous to a brainstorming session, but participants often interact with each other as they react to structured ideas or questions.

Unlike brainstorming, focus groups allow the facilitator to take different roles, such as advocate for or against an idea.

In the world of continuous improvement, groups have been particularly helpful in responding to interview/survey questions such as those associated with the Vision Tool of this book. This meeting form can also be used to generate ideas about problems, priorities, and solutions.

Elevator Pitch

"Focus groups bring together individuals with perspective on a topic and, with well-facilitated and guided discussion, provide useful insights."

Step-by-Step

1. Assemble the right individuals
2. Correctly identify the problem to be solved and develop the questions to ask
3. Ask leading questions to guide the discussion
4. Allow the group to interact as they address the questions
5. Clarify the responses and ideas generated
6. Record the ideas and observations about the group dynamics for further analysis and application

A particularly valuable feature of focus groups is that emotional content can be observed along with ideas and opinions.

Process Flow Analysis

Elevator Pitch

"Processes, not people, cause the majority of operating problems. Process flow analysis is a good place to start identifying production quality or efficiency improvement opportunities."

Many performance issues stem from weak processes of all types, and very few stem from incompetent or negative individuals. Process Mapping is an effective way to identify and analyze these issues.

All business operations – information flow, manufacturing, material movement, financial analysis, executive decision-making, planning and scheduling –involve processes, and many of these cross department lines and are beyond the control or even the understanding of a single person, so a team effort is required for effective use of this analysis tool.

Process mapping is applied iteratively using key metrics at increasingly lower levels of granularity, to define problems at an actionable level. (For example, an 'Add Value' step of a process might lead to a sub-process map for 'Electronics Assembly' which might then generate a sub-sub-process map for 'Pack and Ship.') The types of metrics used to provide focus can vary, but should certainly include measurement of the number of resources and costs applied to each activity, in order to ensure focus is on high-impact areas.

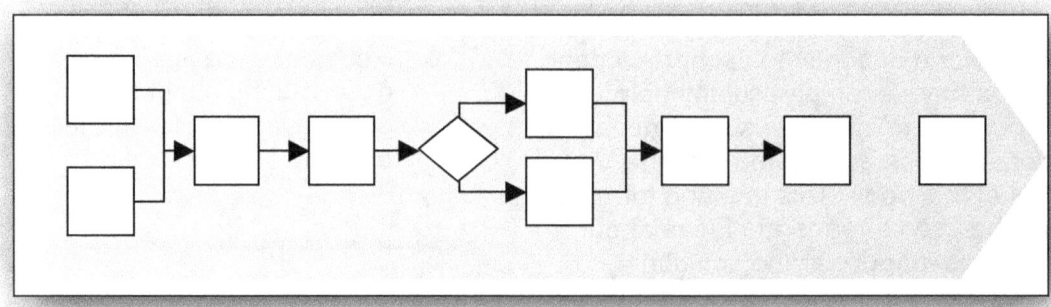

When used creatively, process maps will clearly identify the major barriers to effectiveness and efficiency and will provide input into the business case supporting the change program of a business improvement road map.

Step-by-Step

1. Assemble the correct team, knowledgeable about the processes to be mapped
2. Correctly identify and define the problem
3. At the highest level, lay out the fundamental activities of the business sequentially to provide an overall map
4. Apply key metrics to begin focusing on areas for improvement
5. Develop these areas as sub-process maps, using the same techniques
6. These might also generate their own sub-sub-process maps in order to define the problems and solutions accurately at an actionable level.

Day in the Life of (DILO) Studies

Elevator Pitch

"When you need to know what REALLY goes on, follow the person who does it around and record everything he or she does."

Step-by-Step

1. Design the recording instrument, with categories based on the jobs being studied (an example appears in '04_Operations_Analysis _Forms.xls' on the available CD)
2. Schedule the DILOs and communicate the project and purpose with the subjects
3. Follow the subject and record every activity
4. Combine the data from multiple DILOs and analyze it
5. Create Pareto charts of activities
6. Review the conclusions in an executive workshop
7. Develop action plans to eliminate identified waste

When analyzing a process, It is always necessary to find out NOT what people think is happening, but what really IS happening. That is the purpose of the 'Day In the Life Of' study, designed to uncover significant waste such as the waste of walking around looking for people or things, wrestling with balky machinery, filling out paperwork, and the like.

Multiple DILOs are generally necessary to ensure the sample size is sufficient to support the conclusions, and the DILOs need to be long enough – at least half a shift – to record all activity. It is also, of course, critical that the data is collected in a non-intrusive way and that there is trust that the purpose is to create a better work environment.

Simple observation of random time samples will generally be sufficient to understand the improvement opportunities of simple, repetitive operations; DILOs are reserved for more complex work, such as floor supervision, where every action is recorded on an instrument as minutes falling into a few categories, such as:

○ Meetings
○ Coaching and directing employees
○ Walking
○ Break
○ Talking with the consultant
○ Looking for something

Ratio Delay Analysis

Ratio Delay Analysis is a form of work sampling, a statistical technique for finding out what operators and machines are actually doing. Many observations of typical activities are made at random times, and activities are recorded in various defined categories such as 'machine setup,' 'waiting' or 'idle,' 'walking around,' 'productive work,' and the like. This is a quick and effective tool for identifying improvement opportunities.

It is important to take enough observations to provide a statistically relevant sample. It is also important that observations are taken discretely to ensure the results don't reflect only the best behavior. But individuals observed should not be identified except in cases of egregious behavior (blatant disregard for safety or criminal activity, for example) – the purpose is to identify overall shop effectiveness.

When combined with process flow analysis and DILOs, Ratio Delay Analysis provides a very solid view of the 'as is' condition of an operation.

Elevator Pitch

"Ratio Delay Analysis provides a quick view of shop floor activity, based on a number of short observations, in order to identify improvement opportunities."

Step-by-Step

1. Define manufacturing tasks to be analyzed
2. Define the task categories to be recorded, such as 'working,' 'waiting,' 'walking.'
3. Design the study forms, and set the schedule
4. Prepare the team of observers
5. Make random visits to the plant and collect the observations
6. Analyze the results
7. Present results and develop an action plan to eliminate waste / improve quality

Check Sheet

Elevator Pitch

"A check sheet simply catches and organizes data about a process for analysis to measure its effectiveness."

Check sheets capture such information as the frequency of each type of problem or aberration in a process for each period, or by area of the production process. If an electronic spreadsheet is used, it is then easy to graph or sort the data for insights into improvement priorities.

For example, the check sheet below could be sorted in descending order and displayed as a Pareto Chart, or it might be used to compare shift effectiveness or for other management purposes.

Problem	Monday 1st Shift	Monday 2nd Shift	Tuesday 1st Shift	Tuesday 2nd Shift	Wednesday 1st Shift	Wednesday 2nd Shift	Total
Broken Flange	✓✓✓		✓✓✓			✓✓✓✓✓	11
Paint Streaking		✓					1
Gear Misalignment			✓✓	✓	✓	✓	5
Short Shaft				✓	✓	✓	3
Sticking Valves				✓	✓	✓	3
Electrical Short		✓✓✓✓✓					5
Unknown		✓	✓	✓	✓		4

Apply the Tools to Get It Done

Scatter Diagram

A scatter diagram attempts to estimate future outcomes based on historical correlation between 2 variables. For example, as depicted in the diagram below, it will be useful to estimate how much fuel will be required to drive a certain known distance, or to estimate how much further one might drive given the remaining fuel on board.

Elevator Pitch

"A scatter diagram arrays 2 variables on the same chart to estimate their degree of correlation, and to predict future outcomes."

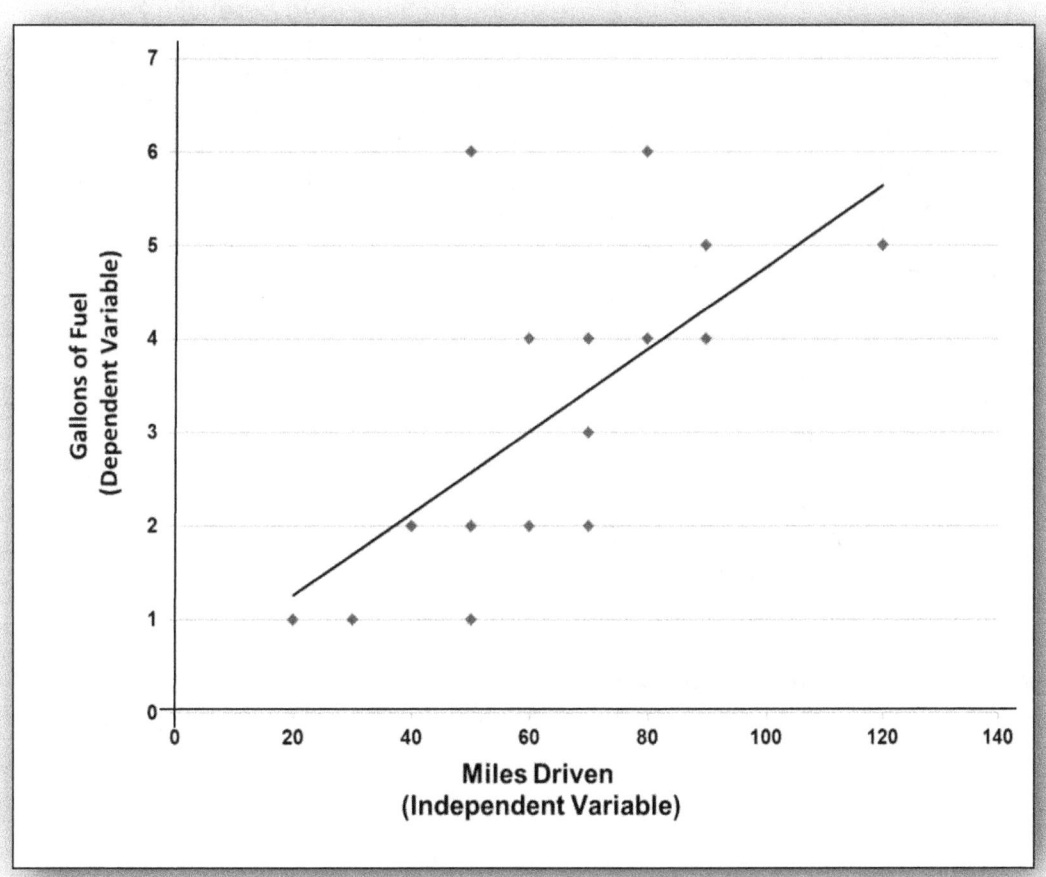

Ishikawa Diagram

Elevator Pitch

"An Ishikawa (or 'root cause') diagram logically connects a problem to its roots in an intuitive 'fish bone' format."

Step-by-Step

1. Correctly identify and define the problem
2. Assemble a team of experts (people who understand the problem) and brainstorm possible causes
3. For each cause, ask "why does that happen" and create sub-branches until the true roots are identified
4. As a team, develop a prioritized approach to solving the problem at its roots

The Ishikawa (or fish bone) cause and effect diagram is widely used to identify the roots of problems by successively asking "why does this happen?" and drawing branches to represent the answer.

For example, referring to the example below, "why are our products selling poorly?" If the answer is that we are working on the wrong products, "why are we doing that?" If the answer is that headquarters is directing the effort, "why are they pushing the wrong designs?" If the answer is poor business intelligence, "why can't we get them the information they need?" and so on.

In this example of an Ishikawa diagram, the issue is that products are performing poorly in the marketplace. There may be multiple reasons, such as "investing resources in the wrong projects," or 'excessive cycle times / cost." In each case, ask "Why is this happening?" Misdirected investments may be due to poor directions from headquarters, poor focus on customers or markets, failure to capitalize on core strengths, or possibly other root causes – or possibly all of the above. Once every significant cause is identified, the prioritization process can begin.

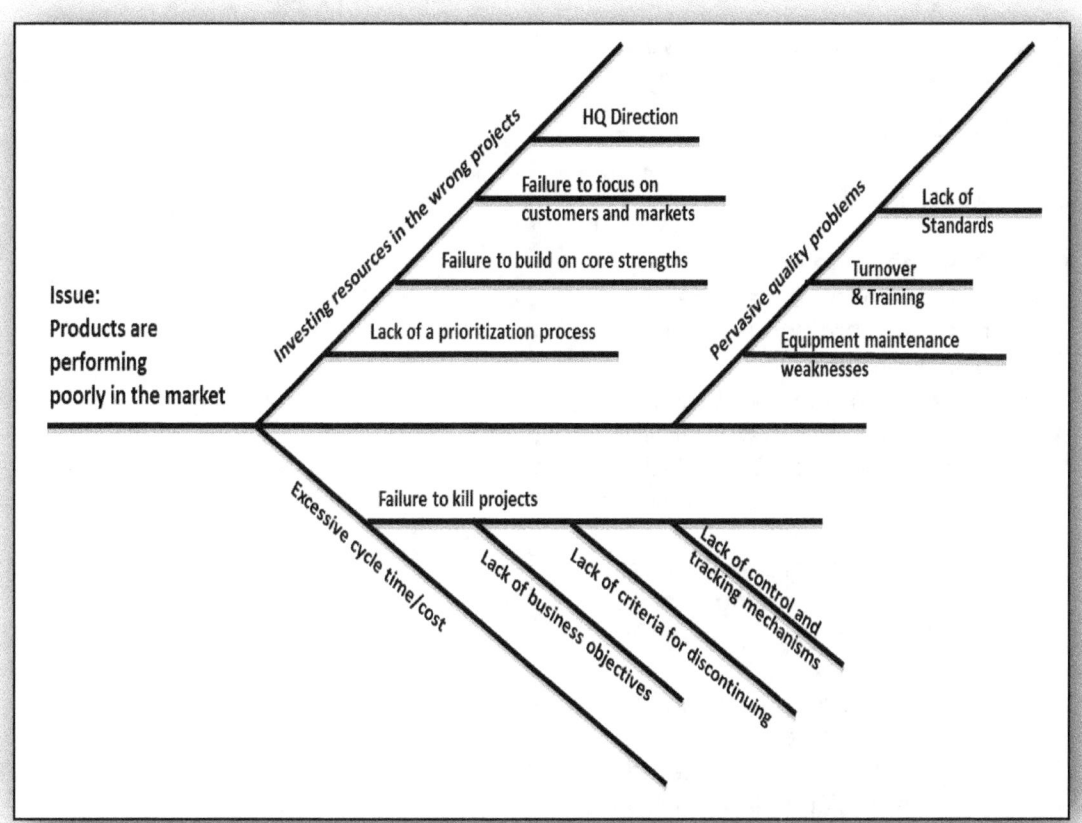

Affinity Diagrams

Elevator Pitch

"The Affinity Diagram helps teams focus by organizing ideas into logically related categories."

An Affinity Diagram helps a team to coalesce around specific issues which may not appear to be related, and to think through where to focus their efforts. The example illustrated might fit any medical environment, and would provide a useful starting point for problem solving.

Step-by-Step

To create the diagram:

1. Assemble the team
2. Create up to 10 statements related to problem(similar to brainstorming)
3. Write them on Post-It notes
4. Stick them onto a wall or flip chart close to other related notes created by themselves or others
5. Discuss and agree on a final arrangement, moving notes as needed to gain consensus on the groupings
6. Give each group a descriptive name or phrase
7. As groupings are completed and the thinking clarified, some ideas may be killed and others refined.

In this example, random ideas have been generated in a brainstorming session. It would be possible to address each item uniquely (for example, to investigate why doctors are too busy or charts are sometimes missing) but to effectively solve a problem at its roots it helps to design a project that bounds the problem. Here, there is potential value in investigating the whole data system, some key processes, and the training systems in use.

A Typical Affinity Diagram

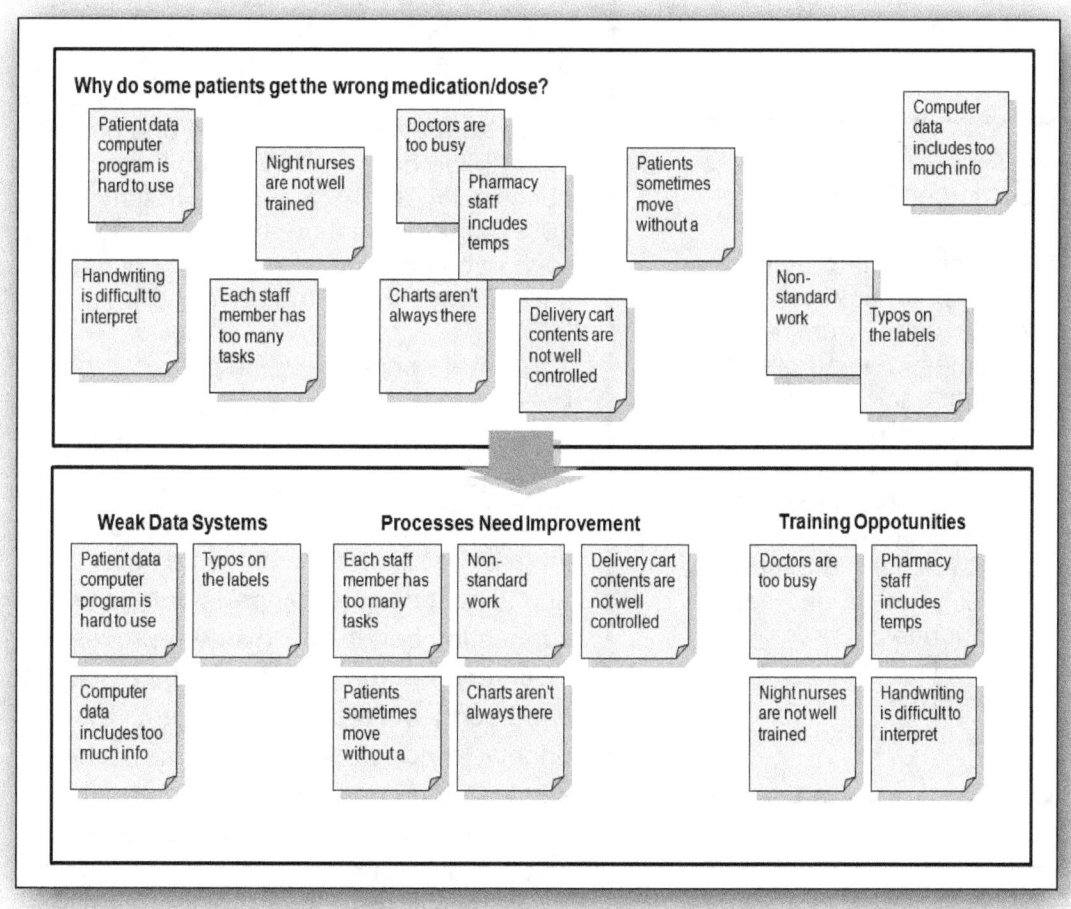

Pareto Analysis

Elevator Pitch

"The Pareto diagram arrays problem sources according to their frequency of occurrence, demonstrating the 80—20 rule (80% of the problems stem from 20% of the causes)."

Step-by-Step

1. Identify the problem and its potential sources
2. Count the number of times in a sample period that each source causes the problem
3. Array the sources on a chart from most frequent to least frequent
4. Consider the ease of fixing each, and set priorities, generally starting with the most frequent

Once a problem and its root causes have been identified, Pareto analysis is an effective way to determine where to start improving the process creating the problem. The concept is simple: find out which root causes are most often to blame and start there.

The Pareto principle (also known as the 80-20 rule) states that, for many phenomena, 80% of the consequences stem from 20% of the causes. Business consultant Joseph M. Juran suggested the principle and named it after Italian economist Vilfredo Pareto, who observed that 80% of income in Italy went to 20% of the population. It is a common rule-of-thumb in business; e.g., '80% of your sales comes from 20% of your clients. '

The Pareto principle is the basis for the Pareto chart, a key tool used in total quality control and Six Sigma. In the example illustrated, a production problem is driven most often by machine failures, suggesting the maintenance area could be improved, and almost as often by parts outages, suggesting better WIP (work-in-process) inventory methods are needed. In fact, the chart suggests a series of projects by priority, although of course some of the suggested priorities would be more difficult, more time-consuming, or less amenable to solution than others.

In this example, several root causes of rework have been identified. The analysis team then reviewed data and made direct observations to determine how often each cause occurred, providing insights to decide the most impactful actions to take.

Pareto Analysis Chart

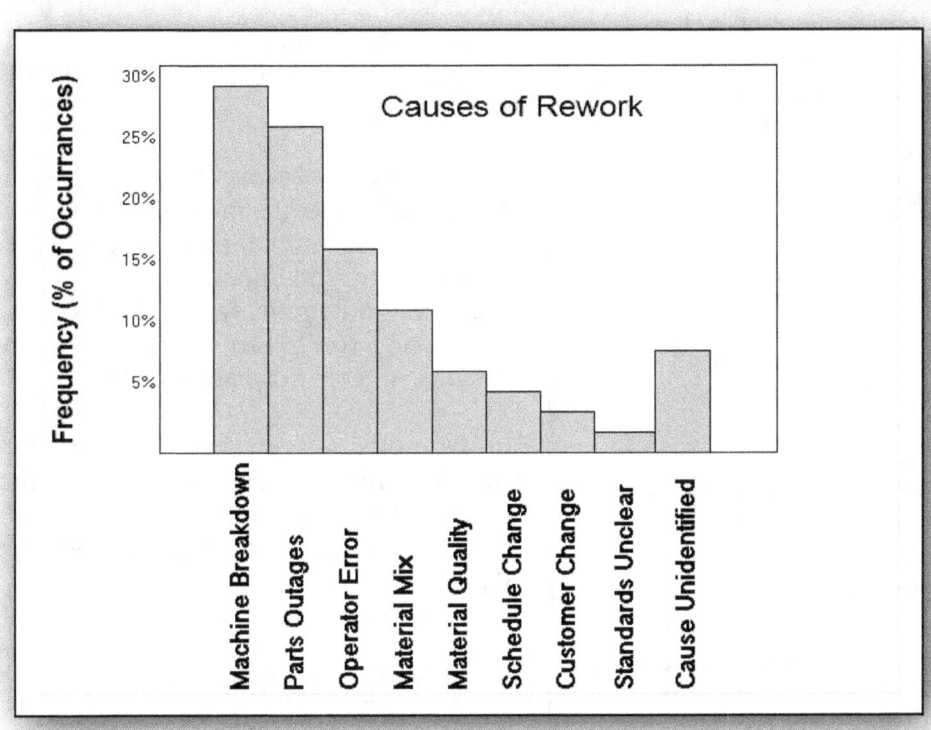

Failure Mode and Effects Analysis (FMEA)

Elevator Pitch

"FMEA attempts to prioritize problem elimination actions based on expert understanding of severity, probability, and difficulty to detect."

Step-by-Step

1. Assemble the experts
2. Describe the parts of a system
3. List the failure modes (what can go wrong, or possible causes of failure)
4. Evaluate the risk associated with each from 1 (lowest risk) to 10 (highest risk) in terms of
   a. Severity (S)
   b. Probability (P)
   c. Inability of controls to detect it (D)
5. Calculate the Risk Priority Number (RPN = S×P×D); max = 1,000
6. Reduce the risk, usually by reducing likelihood of occurrence and improving controls for detecting the failure

Failure mode and effects analysis (FMEA) is a method used in many formal quality systems to examine potential failures in products or processes. FMEA helps to evaluate risk management priorities and to prioritize actions that reduce the risks of failure.

The FMEA process was originally developed by the US military in the late 1940s to classify failures 'according to their impact on mission success and personnel/equipment safety.' FMEA has since been used to reduce risks on space missions and for automobile safety.

For example, an auto manufacturer might want to prioritize issues that might confront their repair facilities, in order to invest in equipment to deal with the problem, as follows:

Problem: Car Won't Start

Possible Cause	Severity	Probability	Detect	Risk Priority
Battery is dead	1	9	1	9
Out of gas	1	7	1	7
Computer defunct	5	2	5	50
Crankshaft broken	7	1	5	35
Engine block broken	9	1	3	27

Multivoting

Assuming the right team (expertise) is in the room, multivoting can help eliminate weaker ideas and set priorities. If the team includes anyone less familiar with the topic, avoid multivoting as it will set expectations of the implied democratic process. In this example, a number of solution ideas to address an unspecified business problem have been created by brainstorming and the experts have used this consensus-building tool to rank order them.

Elevator Pitch

"Multivoting is a tool used to gain consensus among experts about priorities selected from a number of desirable solutions."

Idea							Total	Rank
Sell & Outsource Engineered Plasti	√	√	√	√		√	6	1
Replace CAD/CAM system	√						1	
Install new testing equipment		√	√	√		√	4	3
Develop new engineering processe	√√	√		√	√	√	6	1
New training program	√	√	√	√	√		5	2
Open new lab on West Coast					√		1	
Expand and exploit brand image	√					√	2	

Step-by-Step

1. Assemble the experts
2. Give each participant a set number of votes (typically 5 - 10) to be applied to any item or combination of items
3. Count the votes for each item
4. Rank order the items based on the number of votes

SIPOC

Elevator Pitch

"SIPOC is the acronym for the Supplier-Input-Process-Output-Supplier chain, analyzed to ensure key requirements and issues are understood as process improvements are designed and implemented."

SIPOC is an acronym for Supplier - Input - Process - Output - Customer. A SIPOC diagram is a tool used by a team to identify all relevant elements of a process improvement project before work begins. It helps define a complex project that may not be well scoped, and is typically employed at the Measure phase of the Six Sigma DMAIC methodology. It is similar to process mapping, but generally provides more focus and more detail.

The SIPOC tool is particularly useful when it is not clear who supplies inputs to the process, what the input specifications are, who the true customers of the process are, and/or what their requirements are.

The SIPOC View of Processes

| Supplier | Inputs | Process | Outputs | Customer |

Force Field Analysis

Force Field analysis considers factors that enable progress toward a goal and barriers to achieving the goal in order to develop approaches to supporting the enablers and removing the barriers. It is particularly useful when factors are emotional or political. The following example illustrates what it might look like for a production scheduling problem.

Elevator Pitch

"There's always something to worry about. It is important to get it out in the open and address it."

Current State	Goal
Weak scheduling process drives excessive set ups - up to 20 a week	Changeover less than twice a week

Supporters	Barriers
Executive frustration with sales impacts	Changing customer requirements
Management frustration with confusion and waste	Emergency deliveries
Skilled scheduling staff	Disconnected IT systems & manual handoffs
Responsive operators	Inaccurate forecasts
Flexible maintenance team	Union concerns about reduced work load
Equipment capable of long runs	
Strong sales/customer support team	

Step-by-Step

1. Describe (in headlines) the current state and the goal
2. Brainstorm and capture factors that support achieving the goal
3. Brainstorm and capture barriers
4. Select the most significant barriers and supporters
5. Brainstorm ways to enhance the significant supporters and remove significant barriers

Generic Improvement Steps

Elevator Pitch

"Failure to follow a disciplined process for business improvement practically guarantees failure to achieve the desired results."

There are many models of process improvement approaches, generated by the many consultancies that operate in this space. While this type of process appears obvious, even trivial, many teams miss steps or do them out of sequence, limiting the impact. A typical effective process is illustrated here for reference.

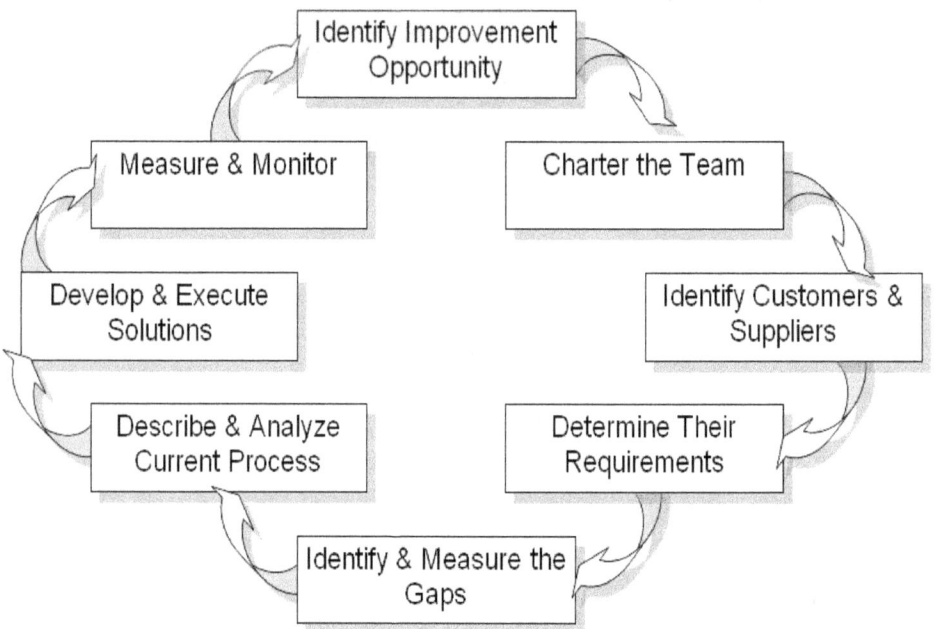

The typical process illustrated on the previous page outlines all of the steps needed to successfully improve any business problem. Here is more detail:

Step-by-Step

1. Identify opportunities in specific and focused terms. Ensure that the problem and its probable roots are clear and scoped correctly Charter the team. Get people with the right skills and experience involved in creating the charter they will execute.
2. Identify the customers and suppliers. If this is complex, consider using SIPOC diagrams
3. Determine customer requirements and supplier needs. Process improvements often drive efficiency, but should never degrade effectiveness at meeting customer requirements
4. Identify and measure the gaps. Develop the metrics you will use to set targets and to measure success
5. Describe and analyze the current process, to identify specific solutions and estimate their impact
6. Develop and execute solutions. If it is a large and complex implementation, pilot the solution and work out any serious bugs before rolling it out
7. Measure and monitor the results, and continuously refine the solution as required

In a continuous improvement environment, this is an iterative process

DMAIC

Elevator Pitch

"DMAIC is the acronym for the most widely used Six Sigma operations improvement steps."

DMAIC is an acronym for a data-driven 'Six Sigma' approach to process improvement. Notice the overlap with the Improvement Steps process described on the prior page. To successfully improve processes, many activities are required no matter what tool or approach is used. The DMAIC steps are:

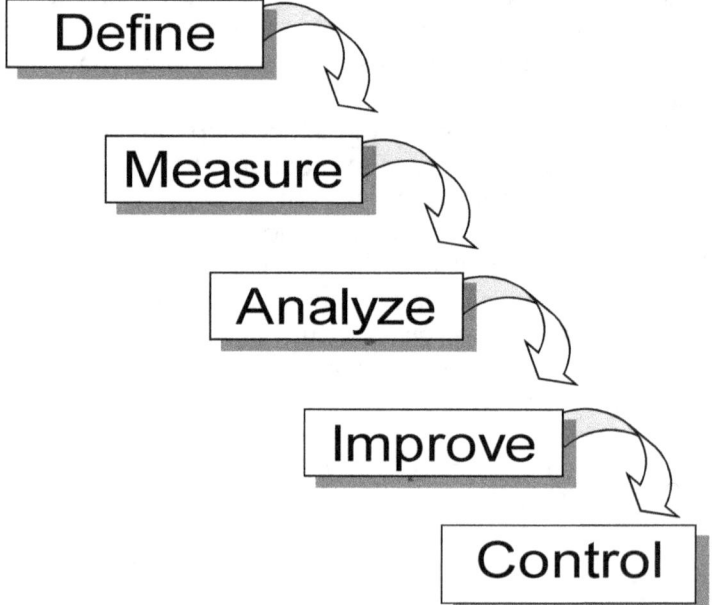

Define

Measure

Analyze

Improve

Control

Apply the Tools to Get It Done

Define

- o ...Customer Critical to Quality (CTQ) issues, and Core Business Processes involved
- o ...Who customers are, demand for products and services, and expectations
- o ...Project scope / boundaries (stop and start of the process)
- o ...The process to be improved (generally by mapping the process flow)

Measure
- o ...Performance of the Core Business Process involved
- o Develop a data collection plan for the process
- o Collect data from many sources to determine types of defects and metrics
- o Compare to customer survey results to determine gaps

Analyze
- o ...Data collected and process map to determine root causes of defects and opportunities for improvement
- o Identify gaps between current performance and goal performance
- o Prioritize opportunities to improve
- o Identify sources of variation

Improve
- o ...Target process by designing creative solutions to fix / prevent problems
- o Create innovate solutions using technology and discipline
- o Develop and deploy implementation plan

Control
- o ...Improvements to keep the process on the new course
- o Prevent reverting back to the 'old way'
- o Develop, document and implement ongoing metrics plan
- o Institutionalize the improvements through the modification of systems and structures (staffing, training, incentives)

DFSS (DMADV)

Elevator Pitch

"Design for Six Sigma (DFSS) is the development approach to building Six Sigma quality into a product or process at inception."

DFSS (Design for Six Sigma) is an approach to designing or re-designing a new product or service with a very high quality level from its inception, building the effectiveness and efficiencies of Six Sigma methodology into the process before implementation. DFSS is also known as DMADV: (Define – Measure – Analyze – Design – Verify).

By contrast, Six Sigma DMAIC as practiced is usually focused on solving existing manufacturing or service process problems and removal of the defects by eliminating significant process variation, in continuous improvement programs after a process already exists.

The DMADV project methodology features five phases:

1. Define design goals that are consistent with customer demands and the enterprise strategy
2. Measure and identify CTQs (characteristics that are Critical to Quality), product capabilities, production process capability, and risks
3. Analyze to develop and design alternatives, create a high-level design and evaluate design capability to select the best design
4. Design details, optimize the design, and plan for design verification. This phase may require simulations
5. Verify the design, set up pilot runs, implement the production process and hand it over to the process owner(s)

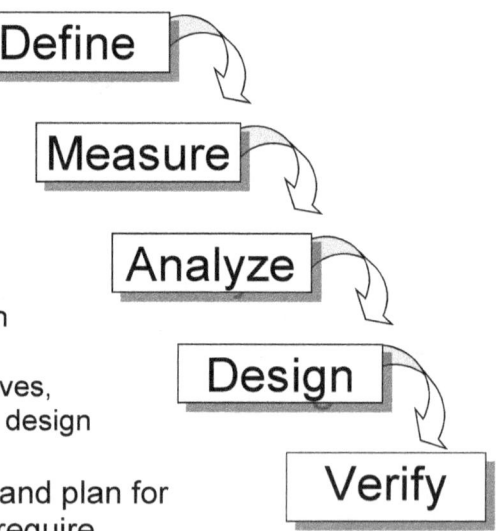

Get It Done Fast with Kaizen

About Kaizen Events

'Kaizen' ('little fixes') is a Japanese term for an accelerated improvement process. It is focused on speed and agility, aimed at producing step change process improvements in a short time and a narrowly targeted area. The focus is on immediate improvement, not long term optimization. Kaizen Events are also known as Rapid Improvement Events (RIEs), Rapid Process Improvements (RPIs), Blitzes, and similar titles.

> ### Elevator Pitch
>
> "Kaizen events are one week workshops focused on implementing an '80%' fix to a discrete problem in a production area."

Modeled after Toyota workshops for suppliers, Kaizen Events are focused, one-week programs to implement improvements in a narrowly targeted area. A team of managers, engineers and operators work together on the shop floor to solve a process problem, identifying and implementing an '80%' solution during or immediately following the event, with iterative improvements as needed later. Generally no or minimal financial investment is required.

A typical event includes 5 to 10 individuals assigned full time for about a week, all with knowledge skills to contribute. A strong facilitator is required, to keep the group focused and to add creative insights. A typical event runs about 4 days, but longer or shorter events may make sense depending on the scope and complexity of the problem addressed.

The Kaizen Event is based on fast cycles of education and application, learning how to do the event by actually using it. This is different thinking for most organizations, and often exhilarating as it:

o Creates enthusiasm for improvement, demonstrating quick results in factory and office areas, internally or involving suppliers or customers
o Provides breakthrough results, sometimes even doubling efficiency, especially effective in the context of an overall culture change (as in a lean implementation)

With practice and experience any organization can develop Kaizen capability internally, though many organizations may benefit from using experienced outside facilitators initially, to ensure success (and deliver value) and to model the approach for dedicated internal resources as skills are built.

The Key Steps

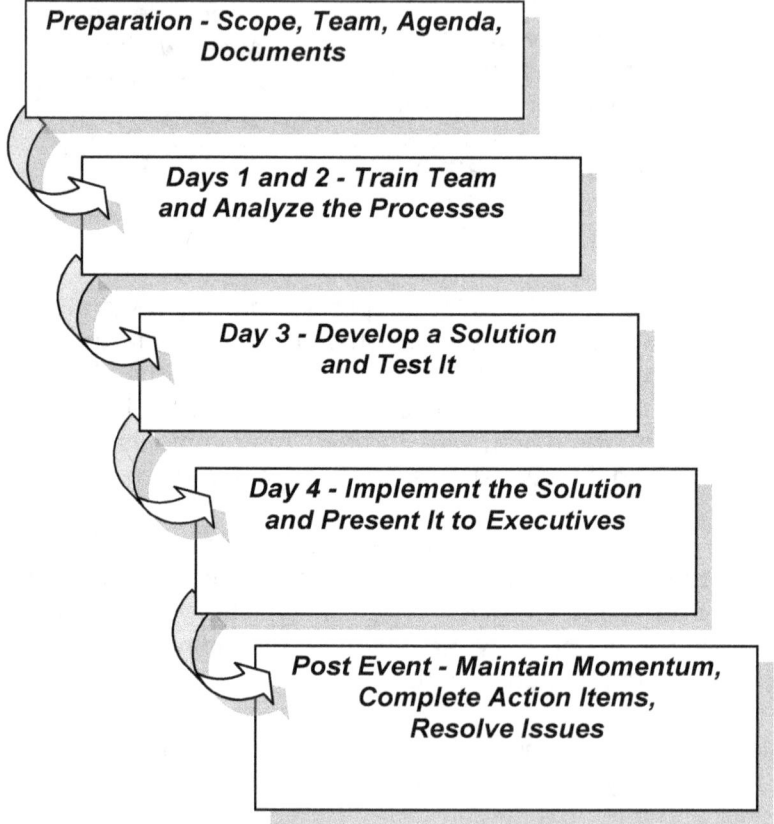

Preparation at least one week prior to the event:
o   Select the area(s) to include. It is very important to ensure that the kaizen event has an area to work in where rapid improvement is possible, perhaps identified from a Value Stream Map or similar analysis
o   Define the objectives and scope. For the teams to have a sense of achievement, and for the sponsoring organization to recognize success, goals need to be set at the outset. Teams often see related opportunities in adjacent equipment/processes, but the scope needs to be narrow enough to ensure positive results.
o   Organize the agenda and materials and identify the team members and roles
o   Collect necessary background data and information

Days 1 and 2:
o   Assemble, train and build the team
o   Understand and document the current process, identifying waste activities or materials
o   Visualize solutions, such as '5S,' workplace organization, standard work, kanbans, etc.
o   Develop the improved process

Day 3:
o   Test the vision and refine it through several iterations
o   Implement - plan, do, check
o   Track and communicate progress

Day 4:
o   Complete the implementation, report accomplishments, and develop action plan for any remaining tasks (who, what, when)
o   Celebrate success

Post Event:
o   Maintain the momentum and attention through ongoing team meetings or process teams
o   Complete action items
o   Resolve problems and conflicts

Event Checklist

The checklist illustrated suggests the duration in days of various activities for the event facilitator. You may need to add or modify items for your organization's events, but this should provide a useful starting point, and should be communicated to the event sponsor and leader to ensure expectations and commitments are aligned.

Activity	Days	Start Date	Finish Date	Responsible Party	Complete?
Area of Focus & Team Selection	1.00				
Select area for event	0.50				
Select event team leader	0.25				
Select team members	1.00				
Establish preliminary event goals	0.25				
Contact support areas and secure contacts for event support	1.00				
Prepare team and support contact lists	0.33				
Event Preparation Logistics	2.00				
Arrange for training room	0.20				
Arrange for event team room	0.20				
Arrange meeting times with sponsor or area lead during the event	0.25				
Establish final presentation logistics	0.25				
Determine event supplies list	0.50				
Conduct pre-event communication meetings	0.75				
Collect any available data and create event data file	2.00				
Communicate event to focus area employees	0.25				
Determine appropriate reward/recognition activity	0.20				
Event Training Development & Delivery	2.00				
Training material needs analysis	1.00				
Training materials customization	2.00				
Training materials production	1.75				
Training materials shipping	1.00				
Training room logistics	0.30				
Deliver training to event team	2.00				
Kaizen Event	4.50				
Conduct event in focus area	4.50				
Conduct daily team leader/sponsor meetings	0.25				
Final presentation	0.50				
Create event follow-up action plan	0.50				
Event Follow-up	0.50				
Meet with event team as needed to ensure completion of 30 & 60 day follow-up items	0.25				
Celebration event	0.50				

Planning Form

Communication is always a challenge, and especially in a fast-moving change program. Everyone who will be affected needs to see it coming as clearly as possible. At minimum, an event form should be created, approved, and circulated to ensure everyone affected knows what is happening, who is doing it, and what the probable results will be.

This example suggests what needs to be approved and communicated.

Date Prepared		
Prepared by		
Approved by		

Event Title		

Objectives	1	
	2	
	3	

Area(s)	
Location of Event	

Scheduled

Week of	

Champion	
Leader	
Resources Assigned	

?

Documents Required	1	
	2	
	3	

Estimated Dollar Benefits

- Annual P&L	
- One Time Balance Sheet	

See Attached Agenda

Event Agenda

The choice of what to include in the agenda depends on the target area. The sample shown (page 119) is typical. Some considerations in writing an agenda:

o   Provide time for an introduction which allows everyone (including yourself) to introduce themselves, to develop a list of team member expectations, and to have the team leaders introduce the operating parameters and goals.
o   Leaders should be given an orientation and appropriate training before the start of the event, to save time during the event.
o   Try to wrap up any training before lunch, to avoid coming back to a classroom environment immediately after lunch; better to hit the floor for an exercise on full stomachs, rather than sitting through training.
o   It is very important to have specific objectives at the end of each day (brief update or a more formal management review). You will need to maintain a sense of urgency throughout the process.
o   Team leaders should meet daily, outside of 'team time,' to coordinate team activities, review day's progress and plan the next day.
o   Keep lunch to ½ hour if possible and have refreshments always available only take brief breaks or keep process moving.

Time		Topic / Deliverable	Reference Documents
Tuesday			
8:00 AM		Introduction - expectations, objectives, introductions	
8:30 AM	Training	Activity overview and waste analysis	Waste worksheet
	Analysis	"Waste walk" - identify and document waste where it occurs	
10:30 AM	Training	Visual control and 5S	
	Analysis	Red tag exercise and 5S rating	Red tag instructions 5S matrix and rating form
Noon		Lunch	
1:00 PM	Training	Standard work and pull	
2:00 PM	Analysis	Floor analysis: takt time, identify pull opportunities,	
4:00 PM	Analysis	Prepare Day 1 Update	
4:30 PM	Presentation	Team Update - review findings, benefits and concerns, plan any required changes to the event	
Wednesday			
8:00 AM	Analysis	Review Tuesday activities and findings	
8:30 AM	Training	Continuous flow	
	Analysis	Part/process flow analysis	People/product flow worksheet and instructions
10:00 AM	Analysis	Floor analysis - refine and identify changes	
11:30 AM	Training	Set up reduction	
Noon		Lunch	
12:45 PM	Analysis	Floor Analysis - improvement of set ups	Set up observation form
3:30 PM	Analysis	Prepare Day 2 Update	
4:00 PM	Presentation	Interim management review of findings, benefits and concerns, plan any required changes to the event	
Thursday			
8:00 AM	Analysis	Review Wednesday activities and findings	
8:30 AM	Training	Quality	
	Analysis	Floor analysis	
Noon		Lunch	
1:00 PM	Analysis	Review status and to do items	
1:15 PM	Training	Maintenance	
3:30 PM	Analysis	Floor analysis	
4:00 PM	Analysis and Presentation	Daily review, identify Friday objectives	
Friday			
7:00 AM	Analysis	Final analysis, improvement decisions	
9:00 AM	Analysis	Prepare executive presentation	
11:00 AM	Presentation	Management presentation of results	

Documentation

Elevator Pitch

"The right documentation will prove invaluable in future reviews of kaizen events, in near term iterative improvement tweaks, long term major revisions, and financial analysis of results."

In order to ensure improvements are easy to understand and adopt, and to continuously improve the Kaizen process, it is important to document each event sufficiently. Most of the documents created are temporary, with only a few permanent process descriptions worthy of formal capture. We recommend an event notebook to organize all of the analysis data, kept by the continuous improvement team in a single hard copy, and an organized set of files on the computer system. Process flows on brown paper should be clearly identified on the outside and kept for a reasonable period by the same team.

Before and after photos are very useful if there will be some physical rearrangement resulting from the kaizen event; make sure someone takes the 'as is' pictures before the event begins.

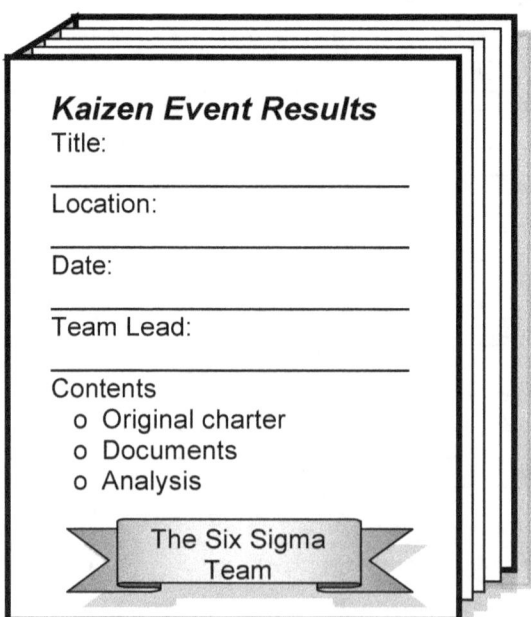

Executive Presentation

The Executive Report Out is a critical part of any Kaizen Event, for three reasons:

1. Preparing the executive presentation provides an opportunity to organize the analysis findings and the process revisions for quick, intuitive understanding. The presentation should be organized to summarize the team charter, analysis findings, description of the revised processes, actions underway, and planned follow up. Anticipating executive questions during the preparation may lead to critical insights.

2. The Report Out is an opportunity to address and possibly resolve any implementation barriers identified during the event.

3. The material can be presented by the full kaizen team, providing first hand insights for the executives and career exposure for the participants.

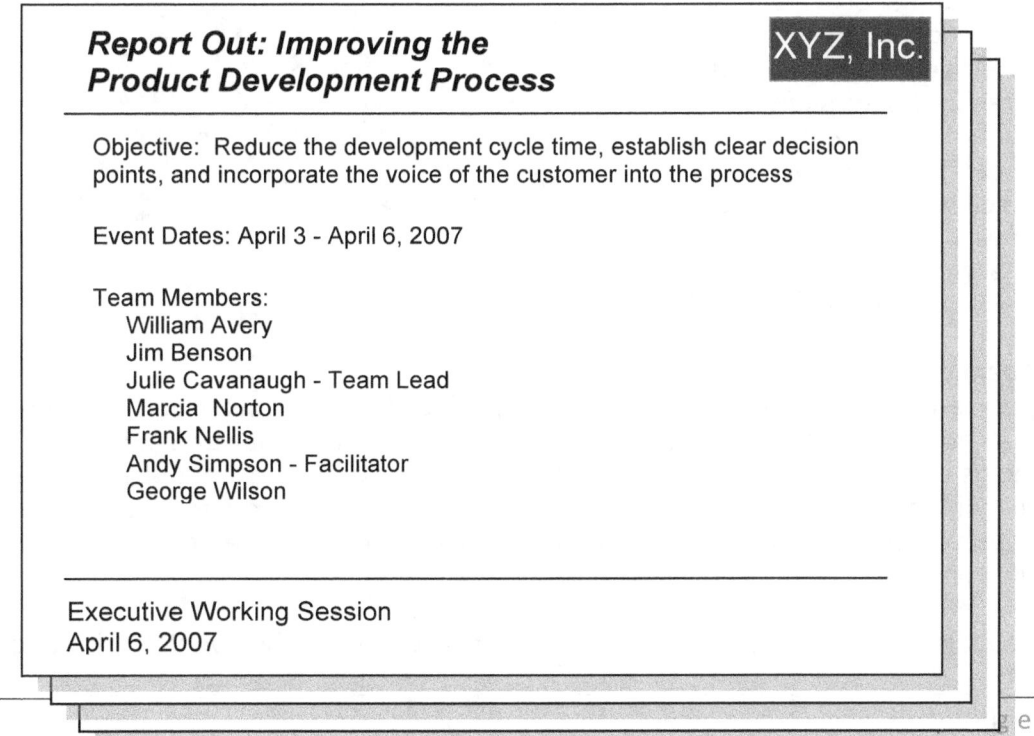

Report Out: Improving the Product Development Process   XYZ, Inc.

Objective: Reduce the development cycle time, establish clear decision points, and incorporate the voice of the customer into the process

Event Dates: April 3 - April 6, 2007

Team Members:
William Avery
Jim Benson
Julie Cavanaugh - Team Lead
Marcia Norton
Frank Nellis
Andy Simpson - Facilitator
George Wilson

Executive Working Session
April 6, 2007

Roles & Responsibilities

Elevator Pitch

"The right team, with the right sponsor, can do anything."

Executive sponsorship is required to ensure a kaizen event is successful. Executive sponsors help the Event team develop the workshop and achieve its objectives. If executives are not familiar with these concepts and their role, it will be necessary to educate them prior to starting.

The Executive team must clearly demonstrate they understand area opportunities, be prepared to define and communicate workshop objectives, identify and provide full time team leaders & members, remove barriers to change by empowering the teams to make change, celebrate and congratulate teams on success, and follow up to ensure that gains hold and to complete remaining items.

The Facilitator - often an internal or external consultant - plans and directs the event, ensuring that goals and objectives are set and that the agenda is consistent with the goals. He or she must understand and may need to teach technical content and application, and must challenge teams to breakthrough levels of thinking.

Team Leaders need to be people who have recognized leadership qualities in the organization. Although they do not have to be in a formal leadership role, position power can help get things done. High potential individuals with no pre-conceived ideas are best. The role of the team leader is to help keep team(s) on track and reinforce the 'spirit of improvement.' Team leaders obviously need to understand the goals and environment of the kaizen event subject.

Team leaders should receive a 'leaders package' prior to the event that includes all kaizen event forms to be used, scissors, overheads, paper, etc., as well as any labor charging information to be used for the event. Team leaders should use the Kaizen 'to do' list form to track individual team assignments and progress during the kaizen event. Team leaders should be involved in the allocation of team members to the teams so they are 'comfortable' with the mix. It is the management team's final decision who gets chosen but team leaders can support the decision.

Team members need to study the kaizen event subject processes and prepare and implement plans. Most team members should be from the study area but the members from outside the area provide fresh ideas or perspective and support resources (tooling, maintenance, engineering, etc.) customer or supplier point of view.

Rules of the Road

Every team has its norms, but a team starts out as a group of individuals. To effectively accomplish the mission, agreement is needed on how the team will operate. At the first meeting, post the following starter set 'Rules of the Road' in the team room, and ask team members to consider and add to or revise them as they see fit; they will more readily accept them if they have ownership. Once agreed by all, these are the rules the team will live by.

Elevator Pitch

"Assume at the start that the team needs rules to interact effectively and efficiently, and deal with the rules as a first order of business."

o   Listen for understanding
o   Ask 'why, why, why, why, why?'
o   Be open to new ideas; focus on how to make ideas work, not why they won't work
o   Everyone participates; don't pull rank
o   Be on time and stay focused
o   One conversation at a time
o   Communicate with 'stake holders' - final decisions are made by 'registered voters' working in the area, whether or not on team
o   Have fun!

Critical Success Factors

Elevator Pitch
"Ensure that the deck is stacked for success. Failure to achieve any of the CSFs is a show stopper."

A Kaizen Event is a significant investment of resources - typically 5 to 10 person weeks - and more importantly carries a heavy weight of expectations. It is very important that each event be planned and supported well enough to succeed impressively. If the following most critical factors – minimum requirements – are not in place, do not do the event:

Commitment from the top
- Give teams what they need to succeed, within well understood boundaries
- Ensure support organization timely response - maintenance, engineering, purchasing, MIS, etc.
- Make sure management is available for team out briefs
- Recognize improvement efforts and results
- Have some money to spend
- Follow up to make improvements stick

Effective planning
Daily agenda
- Prepare panels, worksheets, assignments and articles that will help the team understand and focus
- Specific, measurable performance improvement goals
- Focus specifically on 'how to achieve and hold the gains'

Team construction
- Full-time team members only
- Involve people throughout the organization and from outside the organization (other plants, customers, suppliers)
- Balance organizational levels, functional and departmental perspectives on teams
- Multiple teams, operating concurrently build healthy competition
- Make reporting informal
- Establish, post in the meeting area, and enforce clear meeting guidelines - Rules of the Road

Get started now!

Mistakes Teams Make

Some Kaizen Events fail to deliver full value. The most common barriers to success are preventable. Watch out for situations where the executives or the team...

o Pick the wrong area or the wrong boundaries (too broad or narrow)
o Never develop a real plan
o Communicate poorly (before, during and after)
o Think they are done before they have worked the solution adequately
o Change the plan assumptions
o Fail to follow up (and lose the gains)

Elevator Pitch

"Kaizen events, like all business improvement activities, can fail for a few common reasons. Stay alert!"

NOTES:

Organize a Project

The Flow of a Project

Projects, especially large and complex ones, succeed or fail for many reasons, most of which are related to management. The minimum requirements for success include strong executive support and highly capable project leaders, and a clear, properly scoped plan with adequate resources.

Elevator Pitch

"Following best practices in project management doesn't guarantee success, but ignoring them greatly increases the probability of failure."

Successful large projects generally follow the steps suggested in the following schematic; small projects can often be accomplished with less formality, though the basic principles apply regardless of size and complexity.

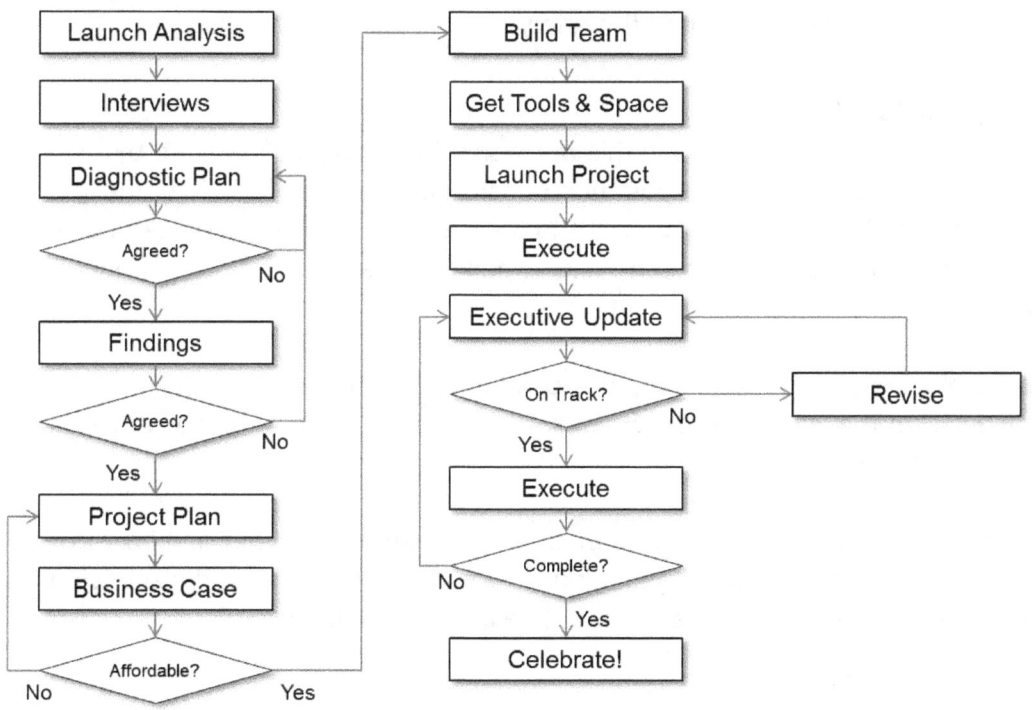

Analysis Launch

It is always necessary to understand what is being fixed and the best way to fix it. The more complex the problem, the more formal and structured the analysis required. Sometimes an informal meeting with back-of-the-envelope plans will suffice; sometimes the launch requires a series of meetings with large internal and external teams participating. It is usually better to err on the side of more structure, to ensure critical participants get the word and to gauge any potential resistance.

At the time of the launch, communications to the organization can head off the rumor mill and ensure everyone knows how to support the effort.

Interviews

It is always necessary to talk to people who understand the problem. Once again, the formality and structure of this process is driven by problem complexity. At minimum, people who manage and execute the operation under investigation can add clarity and direction to the analysis.

Diagnostic Plan

Which of the diagnostic tools in this book should be applied? Guided by interviewee perceptions and common sense, the team can form hypotheses about the problem, its significance, and the best way to investigate. And again, the formality of the plan and schedule depend on the size and complexity of the problem.

In developing a diagnostic plan, it helps to start with the end in mind. What will the decision-making presentation look like? Who will need to be convinced and what will it take?

When more than one individual is involved, agreement on what and how to analyze is a prerequisite to continuing, and further interviews and discussion with decision-makers may be needed to refine the diagnostic plan.

Findings

Considerable work is required to generate a set of findings that are validated and compelling. Firstly, the team must demonstrate that each finding is accurately described, drawing on internal and external experts for the validation of facts and conclusions. Then they will need a crisp answer to the executives' "so what?" questions, including especially the financial implications of fixing the problem. This is the point where opportunities are identified and their potential impacts estimated.

Findings, and the associated improvement opportunities, need to be presented in a clear and accurate way, to ensure fact-based decisions. And the team cannot move beyond this point in the analysis until there is agreement among the decision-makers that the findings and opportunities are correct.

Project Plan

Based on the findings, the team must construct an appropriate plan for securing the benefits identified in the findings activities. The level of structure once again depends on the complexity of the work required, but the content of the plan can be summarized using the 'Project Charter' depicted later in this chapter. In addition, it is helpful to produce a schematic of the project (often as a Gantt chart, described later in this chapter), a calendar, a project control book, and similar tools and documents to help align the team and ensure decision-makers are very clear on what they are authorizing.

If there is difficulty in agreeing on project structure, It is sometime useful to start by agreeing on project principles, such as "we need to lay a solid foundation to enable the improved operation" or "we need to do this in affordable phases."

Business Case

The business case and project plan are reviewed for approval simultaneously, and any revisions required, for affordability, for example, are always linked.

Build a Team

Teams make projects successful by their skillful dedicated focus, drawing accurate inferences from the diagnostics and making real-time revisions to the analysis as needed. It is impossible to overestimate their importance. Recruit the best and brightest experienced leaders with charisma, creativity and intuition, and ensure all team members are clear on the project mission and approach, and trained on the diagnostic tools to be used. For particularly complex projects, the team building process can take a week or more, but It is time well spent.

Get the Tools and Space

Team's always need a place to work, but longer, complex projects might need a 'war room,' where schedules and presentations in progress can be displayed on the walls and the team can meet regularly to discuss progress and issues. Ensure that logistics – desks, equipment, travel arrangements, office supplies, etc. – are in place, to allow the team to focus on the project, not the working conditions.

Launch the Project

Successful projects start with a well-planned launch, in which the key points of the charter are explained and endorsed by the sponsoring executive. Here the tone is set for the team: enthusiastic support for a substantial and consequential project, or just another time-wasting flavor of the month drill.

Execute

Continuously learn as a team – critically review and improve the plan while following it.

Executive Update

To keep a project on track, regular presentations demonstrate executive interest, ensure focus on progress at milestones, and afford opportunities to course correct. Updates should be scheduled at the beginning of a project so that calendars can be aligned and key milestones agreed.

Material created for executive updates can also serve as the basis for communications for the organization, to maintain project visibility and broad support.

Executive participation is always a critical success factor, as discussed in "Get the Team on Board."

Revise
No plan is perfect, and ongoing learning often necessitates revisions. Ensure the team is fully engaged in any change.

Celebrate!
It is important to identify and reward teams and members, for both individual and organizational morale. This is the right thing to do, and it will be easier to recruit the next team when the organization sees that extra effort pays off.

Project 'Due Diligence' Questions

Elevator Pitch

"Ask due diligence questions (like these) up front, and resolve any issues raised before attempting ANY project. Always stack the deck for success."

While planning a business improvement project of any nature, executives should be asking questions such as:

o   What is the rationale for the action?
o   Who will be responsible for getting the work done?
o   Who must be consulted before deciding or launching major changes?
o   Who must be informed to make it work?
o   What kind of information does your organization share in making decisions and coordinating its teams? How much openness is appropriate? How will you ensure confidentiality of critical information?
o   For new products, can you demonstrate convincingly that there are customers willing to pay the prices you've assumed, in the volumes you've assumed?
o   Do you have hard evidence - i.e., direct experience or solid industry data - that your cost and asset structures are reasonable?
o   What are the risks of being wrong on any element? Have you quantified and mitigated those risks adequately?
o   For consolidations, have you eliminated all internal sales and loans? Are all such sales and loans legitimate?
o   Do your cash plans have any unusual assumptions about debt or equity markets? Are you absolutely certain cash will be available as needed? Are banks and stock markets receptive to funding companies like yours, and activities such as your scenario represents?

These fundamental questions overlap importantly with the Change Management issues described in the "Get the Team on Board" chapter. It is extremely difficult to improve an operation without the authorizers and affected workers seeing and agreeing with the rationale. Change is difficult enough without clear objectives and methodology.

Project Charters

Every project of substance needs a charter, to fix accountabilities and set measurable expectations. This example includes the sort of information needed. More complex projects could use this same high level charter, with supporting detail and individual charters for each separate work stream, as the situation warrants. This template is on the available CD-ROM for modification as needed.

Project Charter

Title	*Process Review & Improvement*
Objectives	o Analyze all of our key processes to identify problem areas and develop corrective action plans o Develop in-house process analysis and management skills
Problem Statement	o Our costs are at least 10% higher than competitors' costs o Our organization is frustrated by lack of coordination and frequent manufacturing errors o We do not understand our processes
Possible Root Causes	o Poor handoffs across department lines o Lack of clarity about who is in charge of what
Action Plan Outline	o Identify all key processes of the organization o Prioritize these for analysis based on their significance to the business and degree of problems o Establish a schedule for analysis o Execute the schedule and with each analysis identify barriers to success and develop a
Significant Risks and Dependencies	o Workforce is fully employed, wuth little spare time o We lack the internal skills to accomplish this type of work
Project Team	TBD TBD TBD TBD
Financial Expectations	Revenue Improvements [ ] Cost Improvements [ ] Asset Improvements [ ] Investment [ ]
Analysis Team Comments	
Sign Offs	

Project Administration and Communications

Complex projects require professional administrative support to keep the team on the right page and the rest of the organization positive and supportive. Project time should not be wasted by miscues and rework. Important elements include:

Elevator Pitch

"Lean principles apply to projects, too. There is no place for confusion and rework in continuous improvement."

o The team should always know where to apply its effort, with clear calendar and schedule control
o Executives and other key personnel should always know when, where, and why they are needed
o Employees affected by or involved in project work should also know when, where, and why they are needed
o All team members should know how to contact each other and all work or meeting participants
o All project participants should understand diagnostic or implementation tasks sufficiently to contribute effectively
o Equipment and supplies should be available when and where needed

Communications are key to many of these requirements, and may warrant professional attention for more complex projects. Typically social media, in-house magazines, a library of presentations and film clips, and bulletin board announcements suffice, but press releases and other media contacts might be appropriate for activities that impact beyond the organization.

The 'Project Admin' file on the available CD provides a template for keeping the team organized. It includes the Administrative Information form on the next page.

Administrative Information Project Name]			[Project Identification Number]

Address	Phone	Fax	E-Mail

Start Date (Monday)	Weeks
22-Apr-02	6

Consulting Team Members		Phone	Mobile	Fax	E-Mail
[AAA]					
[BBB]					
[CCC]					

Internal Team Members		Position	Phone	Mobile	E-Mail
[XXX]					
[YYY]					
[ZZZ]					

Executives		Position	Phone	Mobile	E-Mail
[Top Client Name]					
[Other Decision Maker]					
[Other Decision Maker]					

Hotel	Phone	Rate	Comments

Directions

Project Overview Schematic

Elevator Pitch

"A simple schematic of interrelated work activities can make a complex project far more intuitive to executives, the team, and the organization."

In large and complex projects, work is organized into workstreams staffed with experts in the areas under review along with the employees doing the work. For example, a project with heavy IT content requires computer architects and programmers to create and install software, while industrial engineers may work in a parallel effort to improve and align processes with the software

The sample graphic below illustrates a project focused on order management processes. This type of high level view helps executives, team members, and affected employees understand the overall business improvement project and their respective roles in it.

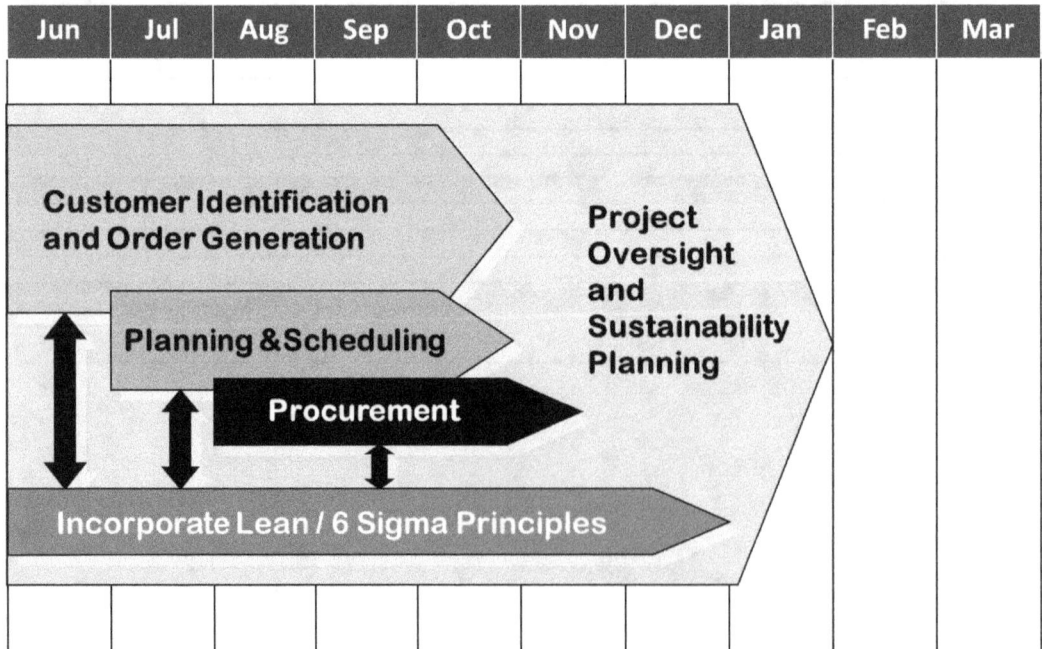

Workstreams / Swim Lanes

In the project overview example on the prior page, "project oversight and coordination" may be complex enough to require its own workstream of dedicated effort (sometimes called a 'swim lane'). Each such workstream / swim lane may have its own charter, Gantt chart, detailed schedule, and similar controls, depending on its complexity.

Here we imagine sequential tasks defined in each workstream, with interdependencies identified to ensure coordination during the project and in the executive updates.

Elevator Pitch

"Workstream plans help organize complex interrelated work, allowing sub-teams to focus their specialized skills in the context of the whole project."

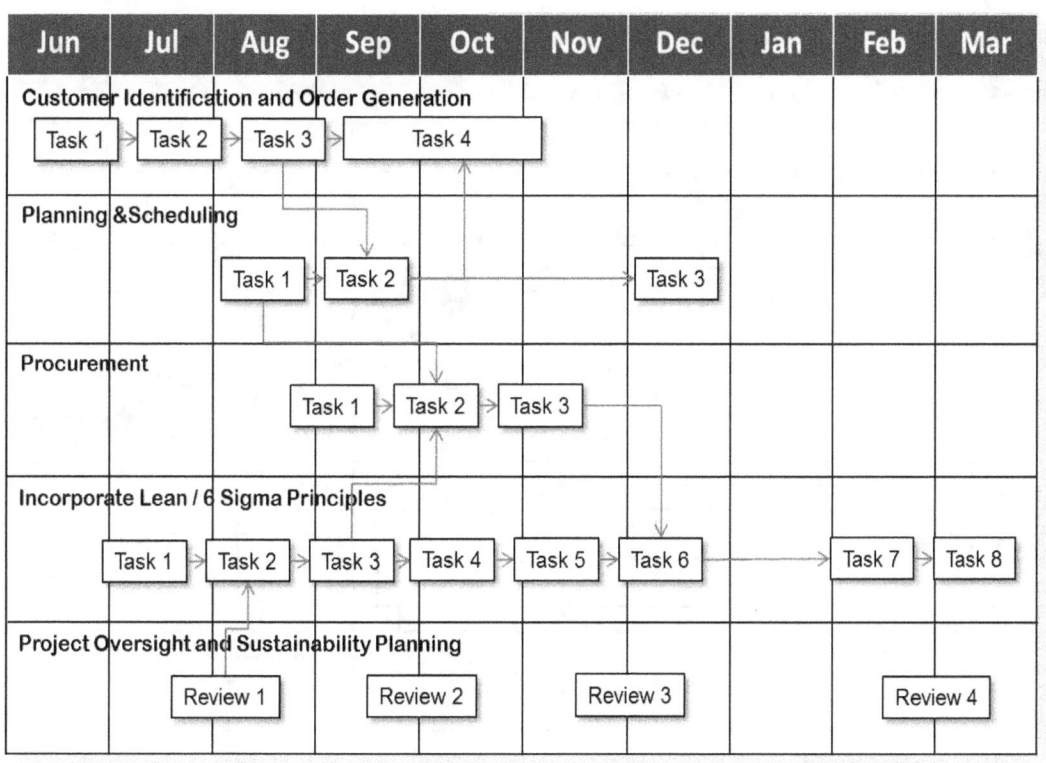

Gantt Chart

Along with the project overview and workstream charts illustrated, very detailed Gantt Charts (named for Henry Gantt, who designed the chart about 1910) can help to understand a sequence of coordinated activities.

> ### Elevator Pitch
>
> "Gantt charts indicate start and end dates for each work activity in an intuitive visual way."

Tools such as Microsoft Project generate excellent Gantt charts easily, though the advanced capabilities of MS Project, such as project costing, require significant overhead (assigned resources) to keep them current during the project; only very complex projects can generally afford that level of effort. The following illustration is of a typical Gantt chart, copied from the 'Project Admin' file on the available CD.

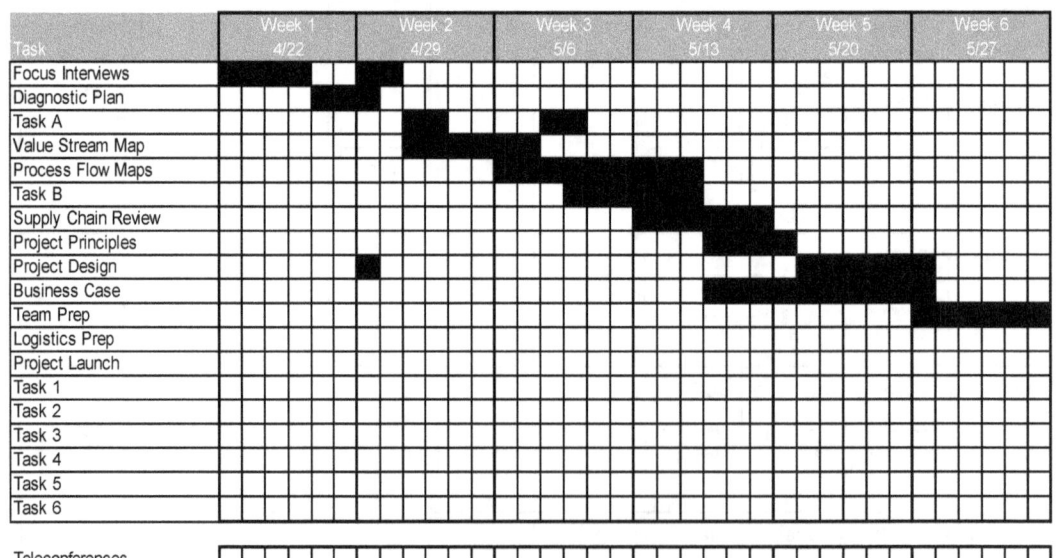

PERT Chart / CPM

PERT is an acronym for Program Evaluation and Review Technique, developed by the U.S. Navy about 1957 to help schedule complex projects with sequencing dependencies. PERT charts focus on the Critical Path Method (CPM) to ensure understanding of the impact of schedule changes as tasks must be performed in the correct sequence. In the example shown, when constructing a house, the foundation cement must dry before any framing can begin; if the concrete pour is delayed, so is everything else that depends on a foundation.

Elevator Pitch

"PERT Charts focus on the critical path to clarify the impact of a schedule change on the overall project schedule."

In this simple PERT chart, the critical path task sequence is 1 – 2 – 3 – 5 – 6 – 8 – 9 – 10. There is flexibility in scheduling tasks 4 and 7, so long as they are done by the time task 6 is completed.

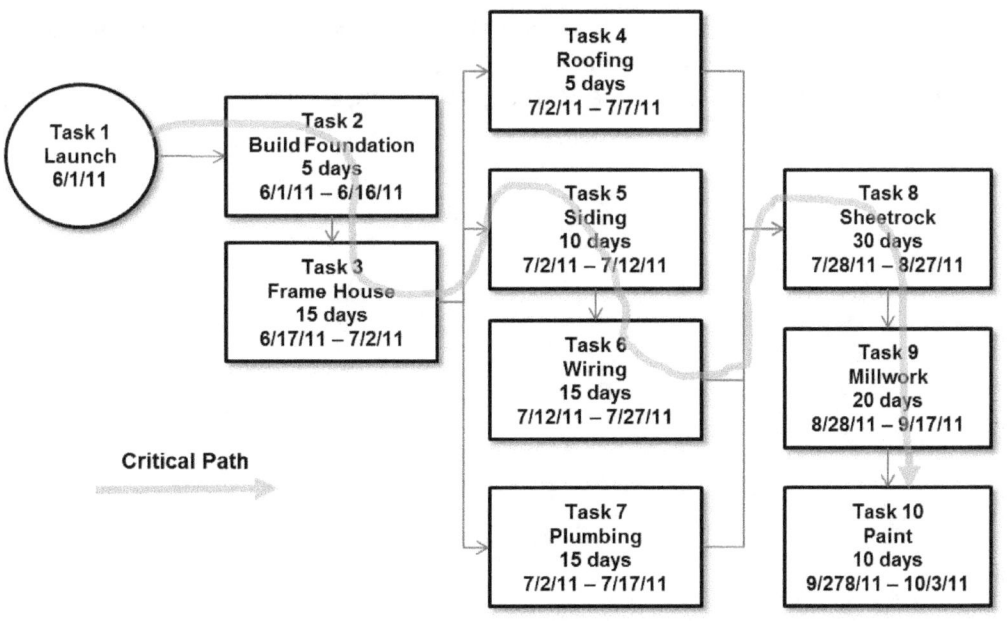

Business Case for Action

A sound business case will ensure that an investment makes financial sense (is affordable and a reasonable application of the organization's funds). This is important for the initial decision to proceed and also, as a project progresses, for maintaining focus on why the project is important.

The chart in the Business Case chapter indicates the cumulative cash impact of a typical investment, with money spent before benefits are reaped. (This chart can be created by plugging values into the workbook on the available CD-ROM.) In funding a significant improvement project, consider:

- o The amount and timing of all out-of-pocket incremental costs associated with achieving the desired benefits.
- o The amount and timing of each financial benefit, distinguishing between cash and profitability inflows.
- o The impact on the P&L, Balance Sheet, and Cash Flow statements.
- o What can go wrong and how significant the risks are. In the case shown, assumptions have been made about the degree of risk, and risks have been addressed by a sensitivity analysis showing a high, expected, and low result.

Assuming an organization has the financial skills required, executives may prefer to see such decision factors as Net Present Value (NPV), Internal Rate of Return (IRR), and other Return on Investment (ROI) analyses, as illustrated on the chart.

NOTES:

_____

_____

_____

_____

_____

_____

_____

_____

_____

_____

NOTES:

Map It and Understand It

About Process Mapping

This discussion is designed to help internal and external consultants quickly and effectively analyze any process to determine its ideal state, and to design interventions to improve its effectiveness and efficiency. We suggest that even the formats described are important, because many people may be involved and clear, intuitive formats will help ensure the accuracy and speed of this analysis process. This is and should look like a working document, inviting everyone who touches the process to participate. Buy in and process change management start here.

> ### Elevator Pitch
>
> "When you want to really understand a process-driven problem, create an 'As Is' map. When you want to really fix it, create a well thought out "To Be' map."

Note that a process map is not the same as a Value Stream map. Although they appear to have much in common – a defined starting point, steps, and measurements of inventories, for examples – they are used for different purposes. The value stream map is typically created at a macro level and focuses on reducing lead time, making value added time more efficient, rationalizing inventories, and establishing lean accounting methods. Process maps, by contrast, focus on identifying and correcting wasteful practices at the level of detail where the rubber meets the road.

Many performance issues stem from weak processes of all types, and relatively few from incompetent or negligent individuals. Information flow, manufacturing, material movement, financial analysis, executive decision-making, planning and scheduling – all involve processes, and many of these cross department lines and are beyond the control or even the understanding of a single person.

Process Mapping is an effective way to identify business problems. At the highest level, fundamental activities of a business are laid out sequentially to provide an overall map, and key metrics are applied to begin focusing on areas for improvement. These areas are then developed as sub-process maps, using the same techniques, and might also generate their own sub-sub-process maps in order to define the problems and solutions accurately. For example, the 'Add Value' step shown might lead to a sub-process map for 'Electronics Manufacturing' which might then generate a sub-sub-process map for 'Final Assembly.'

A Generic Process Map

Types of metrics used can vary, but should certainly include measurement of the number of resources and costs applied to each activity, in order to ensure focus is on high-impact areas. When used creatively, process maps will clearly identify the major barriers to effectiveness and efficiency, providing a basis for designing the future state, and provide input into the business case supporting the change program of the road map.

Creating a Process Map

Process analysis should be done following these tested steps (examples are shown on the following pages):

1. Assemble the materials.
   Recommended:
   - Pink, Yellow, Blue, and Green Post-It notes - 4 packs each
   - Brown wrapping paper - typically 3 feet high and 25 feet long
   - Icons (described on the 'Templates' page)
   - Scissors, glue and tape
2. Assemble experts.
   For most processes, 2 or 3 people can develop the outline.
3. Define the scope.
   Determine the first step - what kicks the process off - and the last step - what ends the process. If the scope starts creeping, return to this step.
4. Develop rough flow.
   Use Post-It notes to capture each step (all actions, decision steps, stops, and uncertain steps). Stick them in sequence on the wall so everyone can review them, and rearrange them until the experts agree that it is approximately correct.
5. Create working chart.
   Using the icons, scotch tape the steps onto the brown paper. Leave plenty of room around each step for documents and comments. Use 'Verb - Object' format to describe each step.
6. Expert review.
   Invite the experts back to confirm accuracy or suggest changes. Update as needed and add clarification. Affix actual working documents to help clarify exactly what is happening in steps driven by work screens or print-outs. Add

Elevator Pitch

"There is a tried and true method for creating a successful 'As Is' map."

Step-by-Step

1. Assemble the materials
2. Assemble experts
3. Define the scope
4. Develop rough flow
5. Create working chart
6. Expert review.
7. Department review
8. Supplier and customer review
9. Expert analysis
10. Highlight strengths and opportunities
11. Organization review
12. Executive presentation.

appropriate metrics, such as how long steps take, who and how many people are involved, how much money or inventory is required, etc.

7. Department review.
   Invite the departments that execute the process to review the map and to make comments according to the instructions - pink Post-It notes for improvement opportunities, green for strengths, yellow for clarifications.
8. Supplier and customer review.
   Invite everyone affected by the process to comment.
9. Expert analysis.
   Have the experts review all comments to identify all key strengths and problem areas of the process.
10. Highlight strengths and opportunities.
    Place numbered flag icons near the steps considered strengths and weaknesses and use the flag lists to define each numbered flag. Place the lists at the end of the paper. Tag particularly useful comments for focus during presentations.
11. Organization review.
    Invite everyone in the organization to review and comment on the flow chart.
12. Executive presentation.
    Invite executives to review the chart, to ensure they agree with its accuracy and conclusions.

Identifying Key Issues

The key issues - strengths to be preserved or expanded and opportunities for improvement - are readily identified and defined if the organization has participated properly. The interactive flow chart methodology of this chapter generally generates a lot of enthusiasm, providing an outlet to air long-standing complaints and to creatively solve entrenched problems. Ensure effective communication to encourage this methodology.

Opportunities (pink Post-It notes) will tend to proliferate in areas of significant problems. Group them appropriately and define the grouping by root cause (e.g., 'Lack of standard input controls generates many errors' might be flagged in an area where comments describe frustration with the errors.)

At this point, also ask 'so what?' Look for problem areas where a lot of resources or dollars are applied, and assign higher priority to areas where focus will provide significant and visible benefits.

Here is a simplified view of a process map, showing the relative positioning of its title, the instructions, the sign-in sheet, comments, flags, and findings (strengths and opportunities). While precise positioning is not critical, It is important to include each of the elements and to make the flow of the process obvious leaving plenty of room for comments. It is also important not to make the chart too formal and finished looking (by creating it with a flow chart program, for example) as reviewers might be inhibited from messing it up with comments.

Excel templates for the common icons depicted here are included in the available workbook for your adaptation and use.

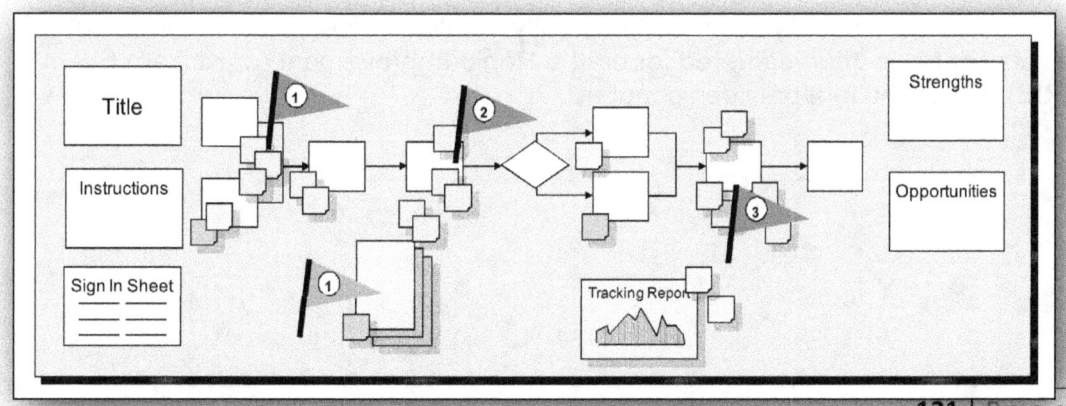

What it Means

The more people participate in developing the process map, the more it tells us. Inspect the Post It notes carefully, looking especially for things like:

o Output constraints, operating barriers such as...
- o 'Do loops,' where work is often sent back to an earlier step for rework. Are the specifications for the work clear? Are the acceptance criteria stable? Are the production processes reliable?
- o Duplication, where work routinely gets redone or re-inspected. Is quality built-in? Are the sequential operators aware of each other's role?
- o Missing or substandard work, with a higher cost of rework at each successive step. Is standardized work practiced effectively all along the process chain?

o The costs of each step...
- o How many people are involved?
- o What parts, equipment, and operating supplies are used?
- o How much time does each step take? How does that time compare to Takt time?
- o How much inventory is held at each step, and why?

o How communications and coordination are accomplished (Attach documents / photographs to the flow chart where they occur, to illustrate exactly what is going on for richer understanding.)...
- o Top-down from out-of-touch executives?
- o Information broadside, with too much data to quickly communicate what to do?
- o Error-prone ad hoc, personal relationship communication?

Greater detail is usually required to actually resolve a given problem, and that level of detail is often gathered for or in a Rapid Improvement (or Kaizen) Event (RIE), described in a previous chapter.

Linking Findings to Actions

The process mapping methodology described is designed to extract improvement opportunities directly from people who deliver or are affected by a process, so that they can be addressed in an action plan. The action plan requires strong links to the source material to gain executive sponsorship and organizational buy-in.

Participants in the analysis process will also appreciate seeing that their inputs were analyzed carefully and considered by executives in continuous improvement decisions.

The chart below illustrates a format linking various planned activities to specific identified opportunities. While the format of this linkage is not important, it is important that the logic be tight and the display intuitive and engaging.

Improvement Project	*Identified Opportunity (from Process Map)*		
	Weak management, delayed decisions and lost opportunities	Confusing instructions and user-hostile information systems	Significant inefficiency due to reinventing the wheel and searching for guidance
Kaizen - analyze key decisions process, identify and remove barriers	Directly Addresses	N/A	Support
Analyze process - flow chart, barriers - identify Rapid Improvement Event sequence	Support	Directly Addresses	Directly Addresses
Leadership workshop - alignment of vision and strategy	Support	N/A	N/A
Review IT as part of process analysis	N/A	Directly Addresses	Support
Review desk procedures and common practices of customer data entry	N/A	Directly Addresses	Directly Addresses
Pilot desk procedures and team operating environment	N/A	Directly Addresses	Directly Addresses

Future State

> ### Elevator Pitch
>
> "The only right way to develop a 'To Be' flow chart for an improved process is with the direct involvement of the people who do the work."

Many practitioners want to start with the idealized view of a process in Visio or similar format assuming that, when the logical flow is made clear, operators will 'do it the right way.' This is seldom realistic, and the more complex the process the less realistic the assumption. That's because each activity of the current process, however wasteful and illogical, is done to solve operator problems.

For examples:

o Information not available? "We'll wait until it is," or "we'll make a decision, send the work on, and hope we are right... or that we don't get caught."
o Quality problems at the customer? "We'll inspect it again and again to ensure it never goes out wrong."
o Line stopping due to parts outages? "We'll keep the line loaded from our secret caches no matter what happens upstream."
o Machines producing out-of-spec parts? "Let's work around the problem with parallel or sequential hand operations."

The only right way to develop the correct future process is with direct operator involvement, not just because they will buy into the new process but primarily because they see firsthand what needs to be done. And using the 'As Is' process mapping techniques of this chapter, they will gain powerful new insights into how they can work cooperatively across the whole process to generate high quality output efficiently.

When the corrected process is stabilized, It is okay to generate the Visio view for training purposes and as a reference for operators. However, this 'finished' map is never final, and will always form the visual basis for evolution through continuous improvement.

Future State?

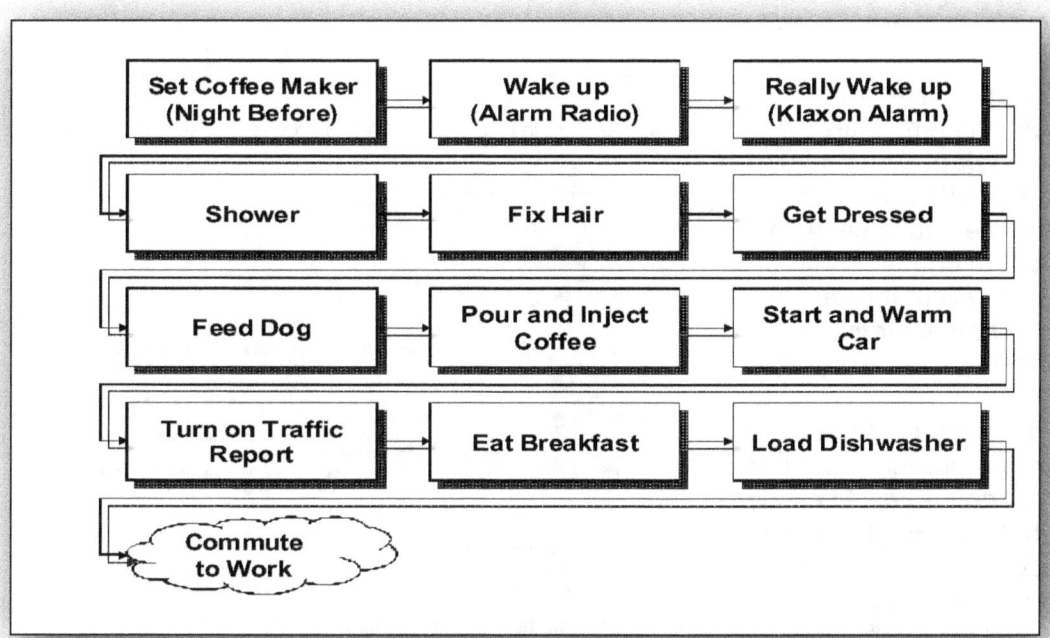

Process Map Templates

Instruction Sheet

The available CD contains templates for your adaptation and use, formatted to print and unprotected in case you want to change them, starting with this very important instruction sheet.

To generate interest and ensure participation, It is important to explain fully what is being done and how to work with the flow chart. Some of the key points to communicate:

Do you work in or interact with this process? If so œthis is for you!

What is a "brown paper?"
- Visual display of a process
- Array of key characteristics of process steps
- Working document showing key strengths and weaknesses of the process
- Low tech, high touch

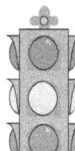

How do I participate?
- Review the whole process if you know anything about it
- Add your comments to the paper on Post It notes anywhere you have knowledge or insights
  - Green = a strength of the process which must be preserved
  - Yellow = a neutral comment which will help others understand the process better
  - Red = an opportunity to improve the process (a.k.a. a problem with the way things are done today)

What happens next?
- The continuous improvement team will review all comments to identify problems
- prioritize the problems and determine where to start correcting things

How will the problems be fixed?
- Address bite-size opportunities in "Rapid Process Improvement" events
- Train the organization in proven methods to sustain fix

o Explain what a flow chart (map) is and the scheme for commenting. The red-yellow-green color scheme suggested here is very useful for rapid, intuitive communication. The energy on the map is visible from across the room, while the detailed input remains available for close inspection. This combination of a big picture with detailed support is particularly valuable in executive presentations.

o Explain what will happen next and who will do it. However, don't make promises that won't be delivered. Employees of many organizations have become jaded by flavor of the month improvement activities, and this process mapping approach is too valuable to be squandered.

Sign In Sheet

To demonstrate authenticity of the process and accuracy of the comments, ask everyone who creates or comments on the process to sign in. This will squelch any concerns that the comments represent uninformed opinion. Executives often look for the names of thought leaders on these maps, and may suggest others not listed who can provide additional perspectives. The Excel workbook contains a sign-in sheet formatted to print.

Process Step Template

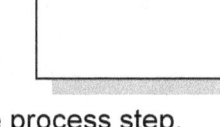

This simple box can include appropriate 'What - Who - Where - When - How' information, but must include at least the What. We suggest that all process steps be entered in Verb - Object format (e.g., 'Attach Bolts') and that any additional information be bullet points only. If clarification is needed, attach the desk procedures, documents used in the process step, resource lists, or other documents, as needed. The Excel workbook contains a page of step templates (simple boxes) formatted to print.

Process Decision Template

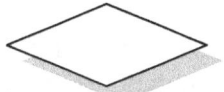

Processes often contain decision points which are often a source of confusion and rework. The Excel page of standard decision icons is formatted for printing.

Cloud Template

Many processes have inputs from processes undefined, either because they are beyond the process scope or because they are undocumented, informal, and subject to change. Such inputs are generally captured using a cloud icon. Uncertainties in related processes often drive confusion and errors into processes, so leave some room around the clouds for comments. The Excel page is formatted for printing.

Flag Templates

As we discussed under 'Identifying Key Issues,' groups of pink Post It notes (opportunities) can usually be characterized by one headline statement summarizing the comments and their root causes. The Excel page in the available CD is formatted to print four pages:

o   Nine red flags to be placed near opportunity comment groups (pink Post It notes)
o   Nine green flags to be placed near groups of green (strength) Post It notes
o   A summary page to write headlines associated with each red flag
o   A summary page to write headlines associated with each green flag

While setting the flags, It is useful to tag specific comments for reference during executive reviews, to demonstrate the link between identified problems and primary sources.

RACI Charting

RACI is an acronym for 'Responsible-Accountable-Consulted-Informed', referring to the roles and responsibilities of everyone in an organization. For every step of a process, and for every activity of a function, a single person is <u>accountable</u> – the buck has to stop somewhere.

That person, or another(s) delegated by him or her, is/are <u>responsible</u> for taking the action or completing the process step. It is not uncommon to find confusion about how work is to get done, and a process map is likely to identify this confusion.

It is also important to <u>consult</u> individuals who are accountable for activities or process steps that will be impacted by process or functional changes being considered.

And there are others, responsible for impacted processes or activities, who need to be <u>informed</u> to ensure a smooth transition to new operating procedures.

Elevator Pitch

"If everyone is accountable, NO ONE is accountable. It is always important to know who is supposed to be in charge."

Step-by-Step

1. Start with a process flow chart.
2. Identify all key actions and decisions.
3. Have the team identify the individuals accountable, responsible, to be consulted and to be informed for each action or decision.
4. Solicit comments (on Post-It Notes) about the RACI effectiveness for the various steps.
5. Resolve 'As-Is' process flow issues.
6. Follow up with executives and managers to ensure any RACI confusion identified is addressed.

NOTES:

Stop Boiling the Ocean

About the Initiatives Review

Many organizations try to 'boil the ocean,' working on many improvement initiatives simultaneously, investing considerable time and resources without coordination or prioritization. This chapter contains simple formats for investigating who is doing what, where and why in order to help executives focus the resources of the organization on the improvements that will really count.

> ## Elevator Pitch
>
> "Large, complex companies often dissipate energy in worthy but uncoordinated projects. There is value in placing them all on a level and visible playing field."

There is benefit to communicating this review openly and up front with the whole organization, and especially the initiative sponsors and participants, as there may be disappointments as favorite projects are revised or killed, and a clear rationale explaining priorities and resource capacity will make it easier to understand and support.

We will start by discussing how to set up for and perform the review and then look at what the forms and compiled results might look like and tell us.

How to Perform the Review

An initiative review is simple in concept but more interesting in execution. This page illustrates the sequence of the activities of an effective review.

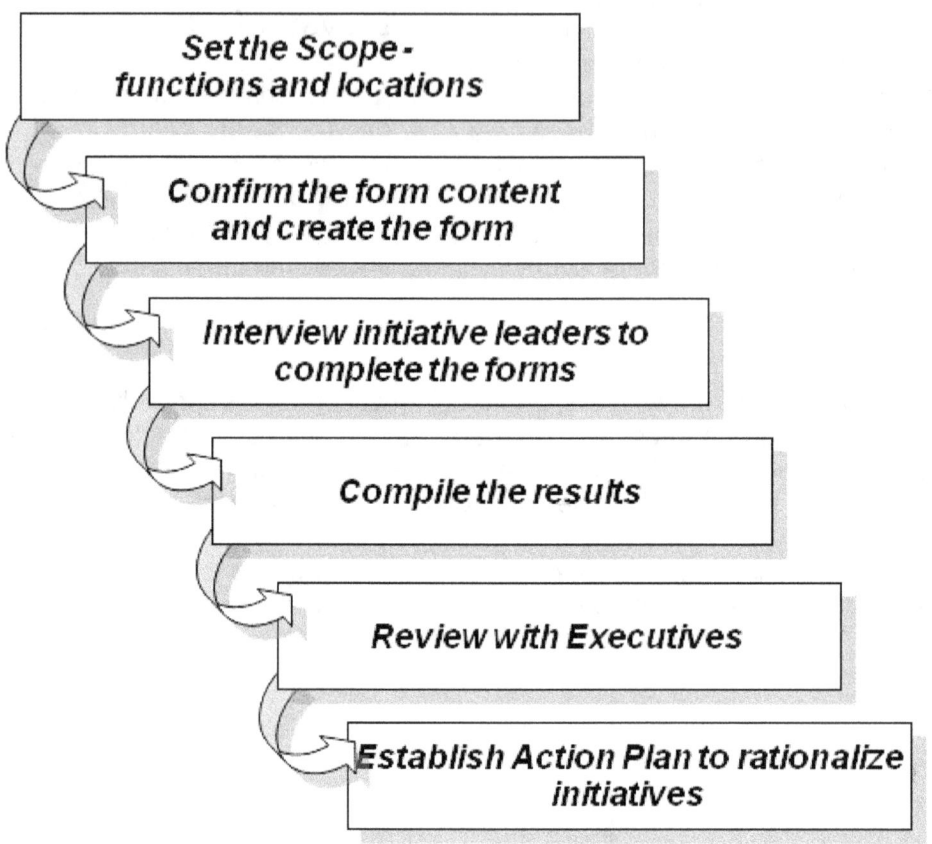

1. Set the scope, determining which functions and locations are to be reviewed. In general, you should attempt to get your arms around every initiative of any scope within your area of control. The initiative review is most effective if it is sanctioned by the executive team and includes the whole organization.

2. Confirm the form content and create interview / data collection / summary forms. Most initiative reviews will include the information suggested in this chapter, but there could be additional demographics (such as business units) or additional data (such as specific types of non-financial metrics) needed.

3. Interview initiative leaders to complete the forms. These forms do not work well as survey instruments because initiative owners may not interpret them correctly and more importantly may not want to cooperate fully. The interview format affords the opportunity to explain the intent and sell the concept.

4. Compile the results. The summary form will capture all required information for a collection of simple initiatives. If interview forms are needed, they can be added to the Summary form.

5. Review with Executives. The purpose of an initiative review is to bring executive focus and control to resource investments, so the full executive team should begin the rationalization process with a formal briefing in workshop format. The Summary form provides grist enough for the inevitable questions and follow on discussions. The analyst will certainly be asked for an opinion and needs to bring recommendations to the executive briefing.

6. Establish an Action Plan to rationalize initiatives and reassign resources, as needed. This will often include executive workshops, creation of an Executive Steering Team, and project charter development assignments.

Initiative Review Summary Form

The form on page 223 is used to collect information about all initiatives in order to compare them and see the total impact of these activities. For relatively small initiatives, the information on this form may be sufficient. For more complex or dispersed initiatives, and those with more impact, the data collection form shown on a later worksheet may be a better guide for interviewing an initiative owner.

Effective initiatives have a number of elements in common, as suggested by the data on this form. The initiatives review should address the following questions, and weaknesses need to be highlighted regardless of politics and inertia:

- o Is there a sound business reason for the initiative? How was it created, designed, and launched?
    - o Did an executive team agree on it and assign the resources?
    - o Is there a credible business case?
    - o Is there a clear and complete charter, including clear metrics to indicate success or failure?
- o Is there an executive sponsor removing barriers and providing insight and support?
- o Are there any resources with accountability and dedicated time to drive the initiative?
- o How is the initiative performing? On schedule? Meeting expectations of improvement?
- o How and when are accountable executives updated?

	Initiative Title	Champion	Leader	Resources Assigned	FTE Hours per Week	Start Date		Completion		Dollar Benefits		Written Charter?	Weekly Update?
						Scheduled	Actual	Scheduled	Actual	P&L (Annual)	Balance Sheet		
1	Project A												
2	Project B												
3	Project C												
4	Project D												
5	Project E												
6	Project F												
7	Project G												
8	Project H												

Detailed Interview Form

The individual project interview form (page 225) is for identifying on-going projects, initiatives, improvement efforts, task forces, etc. that an organization is using to take costs out, make things more efficient and/or improve throughput. The reviewer needs to complete one of these for each initiative they hear about. They may have to do a little interviewing, and should pay particular attention to benefits the initiative team thinks they will get and what they have gotten so far. Just as critical is how the team is measuring or valuing it and what metrics they are tracking. The form should be modified as needed for the reviewer's organization, but should contain at least the information of this form and must be the same form for all initiatives so it can be summarized unambiguously.

Once all known initiatives are documented on this form, they are collected on the Summary form (page 223) for analysis. If the reviewer finds that every possible dollar is being pursued by ten different projects and/or there is little progress and/or things are poorly defined, the executive team should rationalize the set of initiatives immediately, cutting back or cancelling poorly structured initiatives and refocusing the head count to better effect.

Initiatives Review Form

Date	
Analyst	

Initiative Title

Objectives	1	
	2	
	3	

Function	▼
Location	▼
Type	▼

	Scheduled	Actual
Start Date		
Completion		
Champion		
Leader		
Resources Assigned		
FTE Hours per Week		

Activities	1	
	2	
	3	
	4	
	5	

Dollar Benefits	Estimate	Actual to Date
- Annual P&L		
- One Time Balance Sheet		

Metrics/Measures Tracked	Where?	Validated By
1		
2		
3		

Written Charter?	○ Yes	● No
Weekly Update?	○ Yes	● No

NOTES:

_____

_____

_____

_____

_____

_____

_____

_____

_____

_____

Get the Team on Board

About Change Management

Figuring out what to do may be the easy part of making and implementing good decisions. People don't like to change what they do or how they do it until they are convinced it is more effective and efficient, and won't negatively impact the quality of their work life. Most people want to do a good job, but are hampered by weak business models, management systems, and processes. In this chapter we will describe some concepts and techniques for building enthusiasm for change - the right change.

> ### Elevator Pitch
>
> "This is the human side of improving a business and it is every bit as difficult as reading minds. Unless you are clairvoyant, get help!"

'Low-Hanging Fruit,' 'Quick Wins,' and 'Silver Bullets'

If a process has evolved rapidly from a small operation into something more, It is possible there will be opportunities to harvest low-hanging fruit or gain quick wins (rapid improvements with high visibility and little effort). In these cases, any change effort should start there, and successes should be publicized to build momentum for change.

> ### Elevator Pitch
>
> "Quick wins are possible if you are standing in your own way, but there is no such thing as a free lunch."

But some executives and managers have a tendency to look for 'silver bullets,' quick and inexpensive solutions that magically improve things dramatically. This wishful thinking can cause them to avoid the hard (and sometimes expensive) work that gains real results.

Expect to work hard to make improvements and you won't be disappointed. You may, in fact, be occasionally delighted to achieve something relatively easily. But when that happens don't congratulate yourself too enthusiastically. It just means you've been doing it really inefficiently.

Team Building Considerations

In business, the most effective work is often done by groups that see themselves as a close-knit team, and teamwork is a critical success factor in problem solving and process improvement activities, where cross-functional perspectives are needed to find the roots of business problems. There are many tools readily available for building teams rapidly.

> ### Elevator Pitch
>
> "Great teams don't just happen. They are made up of, and led by, the best and brightest."

Here are a few ideas:

- o At the initial session, have the team pair off and introduce themselves to one other person in such terms as position, expectations for the meeting, hobbies, and 'one interesting fact' about themselves. Then have each partner of the pair introduce their partner to the larger group.
- o Have the team name themselves or their project, and adopt an icon or mascot for their team.
- o Use games addressing a serious business topic, that build skills while building the team. For example, supply chain games that provide roles for moving material (on paper or with small icons) can clearly illustrate the power of clear communications in an engaging educational exercise.
- o When teaching process improvement techniques, use problems that everyone recognizes. For example, have the team develop a sample flow chart to diagram 'Getting up in the morning,' or 'Taking a trip to the beach.'
- o Have working lunches with topics related to the business at hand.

o   Have a recognition event at the end of the project to celebrate success and recognize contributions. Invite sponsoring executives and make sure the event is both professional and enjoyable.

And obviously, avoid potentially embarrassing, inane, unprofessional activities of any kind.

You probably noticed that Lean and Six Sigma tools are generally based on common sense, and not particularly intellectually challenging. Nonetheless, they can be misapplied, or applied without discipline, and do more harm than good. Ensure that your change agents (people to whom you look to drive change) are your best and brightest, most charismatic and insightful. Provide this tool kit for starters and turn them loose!

Project 'Due Diligence' Questions

While planning a business improvement project of any nature, executives should be asking questions such as:

o What is the rationale for the action?
o Who will be responsible for getting the work done?
o Who must be consulted before deciding or launching major changes?
o Who must be informed to make it work?
o What kind of information does your organization share in making decisions and coordinating its teams? How much openness is appropriate? How will you ensure confidentiality of critical information?
o For new products, can you demonstrate convincingly that there are customers willing to pay the prices you've assumed, in the volumes you've assumed?
o Do you have hard evidence - i.e., direct experience or solid industry data - that your cost and asset structures are reasonable?
o What are the risks of being wrong on any element? Have you quantified and mitigated those risks adequately?
o For consolidations, have you eliminated all internal sales and loans? Are all such sales and loans legitimate?
o Do your cash plans have any unusual assumptions about debt or equity markets? Are you absolutely certain cash will be available as needed? Are banks and stock markets receptive to funding companies like yours, and activities such as your scenario represents?

> ## Elevator Pitch
>
> "Ask due diligence questions (like these) up front, and resolve any issues raised before attempting ANY project. Always stack the deck for success."

The Emotional Cycle of Change

Major change programs always generate strong feelings, sometimes even sufficient to cripple the program and generate disappointing results. It is a primary job of leaders, including executives and team leaders, to anticipate and counter the emotions, to keep the organization on an even keel.

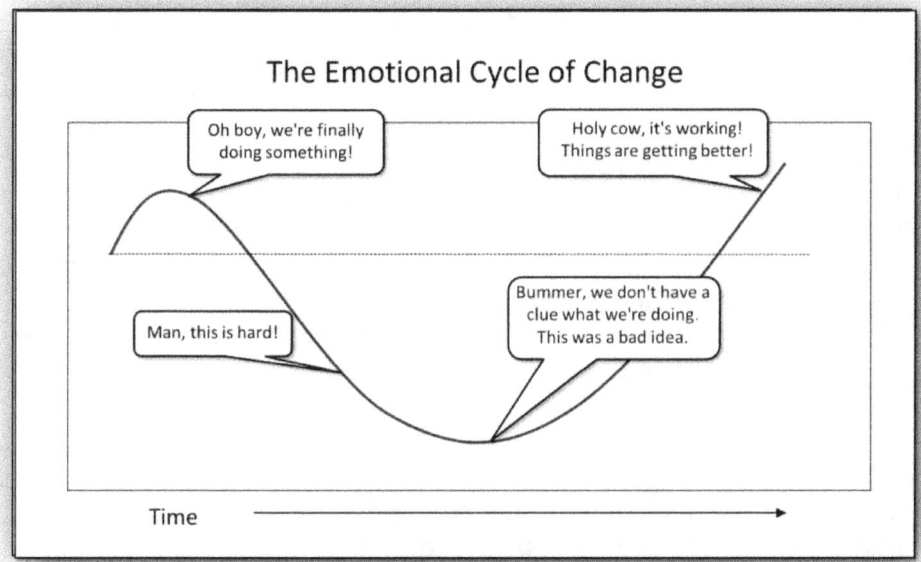

At the outset, assuming the organization sees the program as positive and exciting; there will be unrealistic expectations for the new 'silver bullet.' Leaders need to help the team anticipate the battle ahead realistically. When the hard work of change begins, leaders should focus the team on the long-term benefits, and how much better life will be when the improvements are in place.

In most change programs, people are eventually worn down by hard work and limited near-term results. Leaders need to be cheerleaders, providing for early wins and interim rewards to maintain the focus.

As improvements sink into daily work, organizations tend to become a little manic. It is important to celebrate the progress, but also to provide a sense of reality - It is never over!

Critical Success Factors

Facts - Emotions - Politics

The success or failure of every change project depends on how accurately the facts are perceived, how painful or pleasant the change will be, and how well it addresses the political positioning of all affected parties. This is a very complex aspect of business improvement, and closely related to two other significant success factors:

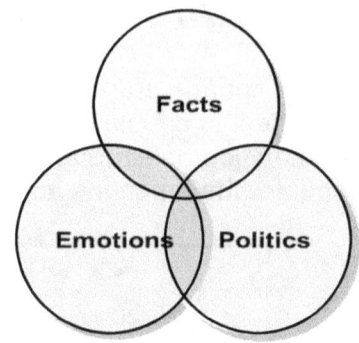

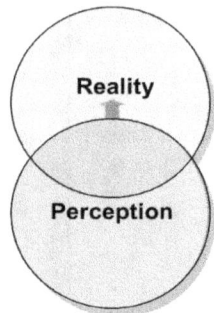

Perception vs. Reality

To be effective, a program must be fact-based and everyone with a significant role must be aligned. The view of current effectiveness must be accurately perceived, and the vision of the future must be realistic and fully embraced. Lack of alignment on the facts or their significance will stack the deck for failure.

Scope Creep & Analysis Paralysis

Projects of all types suffer from scope creep and analysis paralysis, generally driven by managers who lack experience with effective change programs. Scope creep refers to expanding the project to include organizational or process elements not originally included, and can be prevented by careful consideration of the analysis boundaries before launch. Analysis paralysis refers to expanding the data to cover every possible event, regardless of its material significance.

It is critical to consider these factors explicitly in planning any change. Many projects fail, often because these success factors were not adequately addressed.

The Soft Part is the Hard Part

The human side of creating valuable and lasting change is often more difficult than figuring out what to do, or even finding the money. The critical success factors described on the previous page are interrelated and require judgment and insight to apply masterfully. When in doubt, listen carefully. When not in doubt, listen even more carefully.

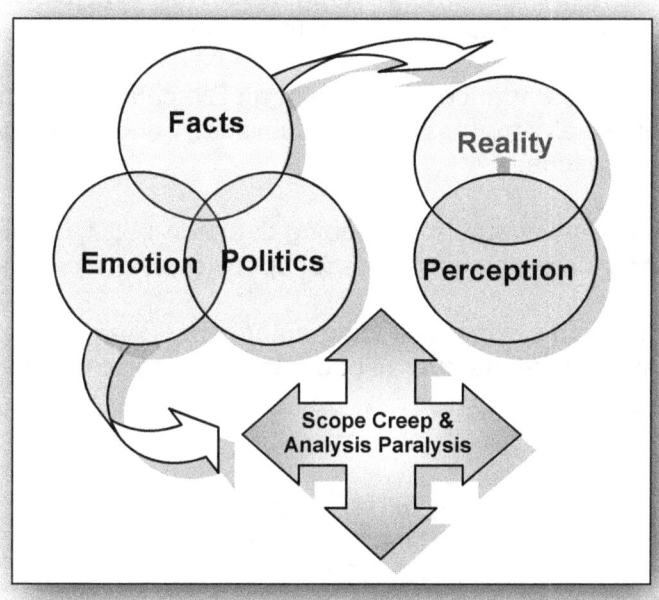

Executive Oversight

Elevator Pitch
"If the executives don't care, nobody cares."

Project and continuous improvement governance are often assumed but not specifically addressed, and teams will rapidly lose focus if the executives do. It is critical that executives demonstrate their enthusiasm for this type of project in at least the following ways:

1. Regular, 100% attendance meetings of an Executive Steering Team to carefully review all progress against published schedules and cost and benefit expectations.

2. Direct frequent involvement in ongoing direction-setting advice, expert input, and barrier removal as champions for specific assigned work streams

3. Strategic direction setting, spending authorization, and resource assignments to ensure success of the overall effort and of specific efforts

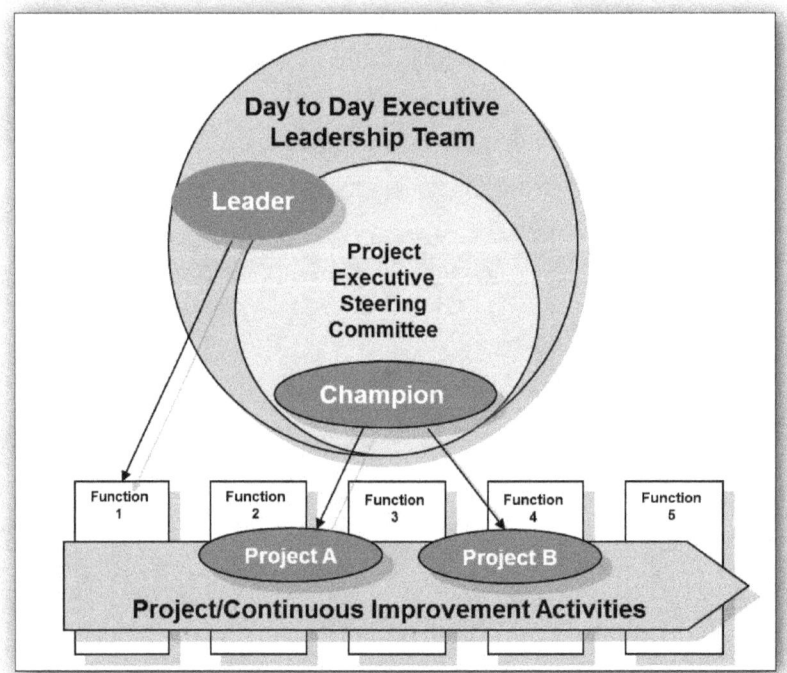

Company Alignment Results

In this chart, based on ratings by each participant in the Vision Tool survey, black indicates significant disagreement with the other participants, light gray is some disagreement, and darker gray is general agreement. Significant disagreement about priorities can sabotage change efforts - there are many ways to resist change, and belief that a project is misdirected is a powerful incentive to resist. In the event that significant differences exist, it will be important to achieve consensus, especially among decision makers, before launching an improvement initiative.

Respondent	Business Intelligence	Voice of the Customer	Strategic Direction	Financial Management	Capital Investments	Organization Structure	Decision Making Processes	Communications & Alignment	Human Relations Policy & Practice	Executive Sponsorship
1										
2										
3										
4										
5										
6										
7										
8										
9										
10										
11										
12										
13										
14										
15										
16										
17										
18										
19										

Are They Ready for Change?

Organizational culture will determine the success or failure of a change program. Some organizations isolate and destroy change agents and reject anything new; others are more adaptive. This quick survey provides a high-level view of change determinants. Few organizations will exhibit all of the tendencies at either the left (overly conservative) or the right (overly flexible) end of the scale, but a realistic view will help in positioning a change program for success. This survey appears in the available CD-ROM Surveys file, and a typical result chart appears on the next page.

"Rate your company along the following dimensions:"

	1	2	3	4	5	
All Talk						All Action
Complacent						Too Impatient
Too Frugal						Wasteful
Rigid Planning						Ad Hoc
Profit Compelled						Customer Compelled
Rigid Standards						Inconsistency
Data Driven						Instinct Driven
Non-learning						Fad Driven
Bureaucratic						Unstructured
Too People Orientation						Too Task Oriented
Hero Dependent						Overuse of Teams
Too Much Consensus						Dictatorship
Homogeneity						Detrimental Diversity
Functional Silos						Process Tunnels

Change Readiness Index

An organization with a healthy culture will tend to rate itself in the center of this Culture Profile chart, with few extreme traits. Extreme traits, when they do appear, need to be addressed to ensure the success of an improvement project. In fact, extreme traits may be detrimental in day-to-day operations and may be worthy of a change program in their own right.

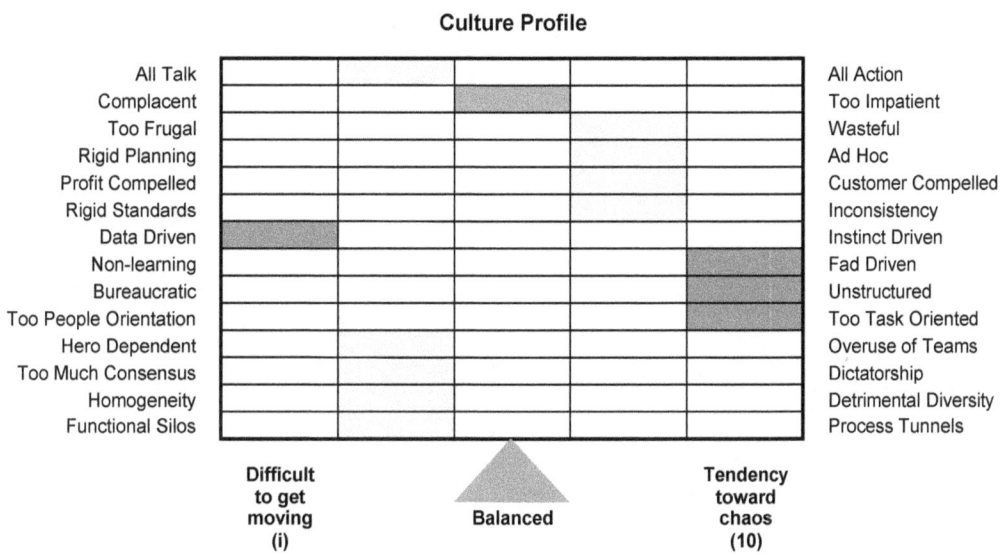

Culture Profile

All Talk					All Action
Complacent					Too Impatient
Too Frugal					Wasteful
Rigid Planning					Ad Hoc
Profit Compelled					Customer Compelled
Rigid Standards					Inconsistency
Data Driven					Instinct Driven
Non-learning					Fad Driven
Bureaucratic					Unstructured
Too People Orientation					Too Task Oriented
Hero Dependent					Overuse of Teams
Too Much Consensus					Dictatorship
Homogeneity					Detrimental Diversity
Functional Silos					Process Tunnels

Difficult to get moving (i) — Balanced — Tendency toward chaos (10)

Implementation of change is always a challenge, regardless of the clarity of the problem and its solution. Before launching an improvement program, review this simple checklist:

☐   Is there consensus on how the business is currently operating, and how it needs to operate to succeed? Does everyone understand this framework?

☐   Have problems (opportunities) been identified and clarified with facts? Is there consensus of all significant participants about what to work on?

☐   Has the organization created a program road map, business case, and charters and have all significant players bought in?

☐   Has the minefield of competing insights and personal interests, aspirations, and biases that make implementation so challenging been adequately addressed?

Notice that all of these improvement steps address the human aspect of change. That's because nothing happens unless and until people act. Even when change is a dire necessity – even a matter of survival – and even when the plan is flawless and elegant, it remains critical that the people affected buy in and drive it.

NOTES:

_____

_____

_____

_____

_____

_____

_____

_____

_____

_____

_____

Index

Sources

1. Lareau, William, *Office Kaizen*, 2003, Quality Press, Milwaukee, WI, pp. 22-38
2. Wikipedia.com, "Theory of Constraints," retrieved May 4, 2011
3. Goldratt, Eliyahu M.. *Theory of Constraints*, 1999, North River Press' Great Barrington, MA
4. http://www.shmula.com/category/lean/poka-yoke/, retrieved May 4, 2011
5. Crosby, Philip, *Quality Is Free: The Art of Making Quality Certain*, 1980, Mentor Press, Seattle, WA
6. Beck, Kent, et al. (2001), "Manifesto for Agile Software Development," Agile Alliance. http://agilemanifesto.org/
7. W. Edward Deming. This photo is copyrighted (or assumed to be copyrighted) and unlicensed. It is believed that the use of this work to illustrate this famous individual where no free equivalent is available or could be created that would adequately provide the same image qualifies as fair use under United States copyright law.
8. Ishikawa, Kaoru, *What is Total Quality Control? the Japanese Way*, 1985, Prentice Hall, Englewood Cliffs, NJ
9. Main, Jeremy, Langan, Patricia A., August 18, 1986, "Under the Spell of the Quality Gurus" *Fortune Magazine*, pp. 22-23
10. http://www.shainin.com, retrieved May 4, 2011
11. National Institute of Standards and Technology: *NIST/SEMATECH e-Handbook of Statistical Methods*, http://www.itl.nist.gov/div898/handbook/section4/prc43.htm, May 4, 2011

Further Reading

Baggaley, Bruce and Maskell, Brian, *Practical Lean Accounting*, 2004, Productivity Press, New York, NY

Breyfogle, Forrest W. III, 1999, *Implementing Six Sigma: Smarter Solutions Using Statistical Methods*, 1999, John Wiley & Sons, New York, NY.

Helfert, Erich A., *Techniques of Financial Analysis*, 1967, Richard D. Irwin, Inc., Homewood, IL

Ishikawa, Kaoru, *Introduction to Quality Control*, 1990, Productivity Press, New York, NY

Kaplan, Robert S. and Norton, David P., 1992, "The balanced scorecard: measures that drive performance", Harvard Business Review Jan – Feb pp. 71–80

Lareau, William, Lean Leadership, 2000, Tower II Press, Carmel, IN

Shingo, Shigeo, *A Study of the Toyota Production System from an Industrial Engineering Viewpoint*, 1989, Productivity Press, New York, NY

Siegel, Joel G. and Shim, Jae K., *Accounting Handbook, Second Edition*, 1995, Barron's Educational Series, Hauppau, NY

Continuous Improvement Glossary

The terms in this glossary are used in typical business improvement activities.

3	
3P	Production Preparation Process. Rapidly designing production processes and equipment to ensure capability, built-in quality, productivity, and Takt-Flow-Pull. The Production Preparation Process minimizes resources needed such as capital, tooling, space, inventory, and time.
3Ds	Working conditions or jobs that are Dirty, Dangerous, or Difficult.
3 Elements of Demand	Customers look for Quality, Cost, and Delivery.
3 Principles of Kaizen	1. Go to the shop floor (gemba), 2. Work with the actual product (gembutsu), and 3. Get the facts (genjitsu).
3 Elements of Just In Time (JIT)	1. Takt time 2. Flow production, and 3. The downstream pull system.
4	
Crosby's 4 Absolutes	1. The definition of quality is conformance to requirements (10% to specs, 90% to customer requirements) 2. The system for causing quality is called 'prevention' 3. The performance standard for quality is zero defects 4. The measurement of quality is the price of nonconformance
5	
5Ms of	Man, Machine, Material, Method, and Measure.

Production	
5S Principles	Japanese words, , , , and 1. Sort (seiri – organize) 2. Straighten or simplify (seiton – arrange) 3. Sweep or scrub (seiso – clean) 4. Standardize (seiketsu – consistent organization / methods) 5. Self-discipline or sustain (shitsuke – make 5S a habit).
5 Whys	Find the root cause of problems by asking `why?' five times (or as often as necessary) for causes of causes.
7	
7 Production Wastes	Taiichi Ohno's original catalog of the wastes commonly found in physical production are: 1. Overproduction (ahead of demand) 2. Transportation (unnecessary transport of materials) 3. Motion (over processing of parts due to poor tool and product design), 4. Waiting (for the next processing stop) 5. Processing (unnecessary movement by employees during the course of their work) 6. Inventory (more than the absolute minimum), and 7. Defects (production of defective parts).
10	
Juran's 10 Directives for Management	1. Build awareness for the need and opportunity for improvement 2. Set goals for improvement 3. Organize people to reach the goals 4. Provide training throughout the organization 5. Carry out projects to solve problems 6. Report progress 7. Give recognition

	8. Communicate goals 9. Keep score 10.Maintain momentum by making annual improvement part of the regular systems and processes of the company
14	
Deming's 14 Points	1. Create constancy of purpose 2. Adopt the new philosophy (of quality) 3. Cease dependence on mass inspection to achieve quality 4. End the practice of awarding business on the basis of price alone 5. Improve constantly and forever the system of production and service 6. Institute training on the job 7. Institute leadership 8. Drive out fear 9. Break down barriers between departments 10.Eliminate slogans, exhortations, and targets for the work force 11.Eliminate work standards on the factory floor and eliminate management by objectives as practiced 12.Remove barriers that rob employees of pride of workmanship 13.Institute a vigorous program of education and self-improvement 14.Put everybody to work to accomplish the transformation
Crosby's 14 Points	1. Management commitment 2. Quality improvement trams 3. Measurement 4. Cost of Quality (COQ) 5. Quality awareness 6. Corrective action 7. Zero defects planning

	8. Employee education 9. Zero defects day 10.Goal setting 11.Error cause removal 12.Recognition 13.Quality councils 14.Do it all over again
A	
Abnormality Management	Being able to see and quickly take action to correct abnormalities (any straying from Standard Work). This is the goal of standardization and visual management. Continuous waste elimination and problem solving through kaizen are only possible when the abnormalities are visible.
Affinity Diagram	A visual display of cards with random ideas grouped by topic under heading cards to provide insights into areas for focus.
Andon Board	A visual control device in a production area, typically a lighted overhead display or board, giving the current status of the production system and alerting team members to emerging problems or abnormal situations.
Autonomation	Semi-automatic processes where operators and machines work together as production partners.
B	
Back flush	The process of automatically decrementing perpetual inventory records, based on the bill of materials of a given product and shipment records. Back flushing eliminates some complex inventory valuation procedures.
Balanced Plant	A plant where resource capacities are balanced with market demand
Balanced Production	All operations or cells produce in the same cycle time, at or less than Takt time.

Glossary

Batch Production	A 'Push' system of production where resources are provided to the consumer based on forecasts or schedules. This may be driven by time-consuming / expensive set-up or start-up procedures.
Batch-and-Queue	Producing more than one piece of an item and then moving those items forward to the next operation before that are all actually needed there. Thus, items need to wait in a queue.
Benchmarking	The process of measuring products, services, and practices against those of leading companies.
Best-in-Class	A best-known example of performance in a particular operation. One needs to define both the class and the operation to avoid using the term loosely.
Black Belt	Title given to a highly qualified process improvement facilitator, particularly associated with experienced Six Sigma team members at GE and its emulators.
Blitz	A fast and focused process for improving some component of business.
Breakthrough Objectives	Imaginative, stretch objectives providing significant competitive advantages and requiring significant change in an organization.
Brownfield	An existing and operating production facility.
Bottleneck	Anything that limits the throughput of a process.
C	
Catch-Ball	A series of discussion between managers and their employees during which data, ideas, and analysis are thrown like a ball. This opens productive dialogue throughout the entire company.
Cause and Effect Diagram	A problem-solving tool used to establish relationships between effects and multiple causes and sub-causes. Also known as an 'Ishikawa' or 'fishbone' diagram.
CEDAC	An acronym for 'Cause and Effect Diagram with the Addition of Cards.' Problem solving team members are given note cards to capture and array their

	thoughts.
Cells	Semi-autonomous and multi-skilled teams who manufacture complete products or complex components in one location.
Cellular Manufacturing / Cells	Grouping work to take advantage of the similarity between parts through standardization and common processing.
Chaku-Chaku	A production line where the operator loads the part into the first machine and it is automatically passed from one machine to the next without operator involvement.
Change Agent	An individual who sees and brings to reality a new way of doing business.
Changeover	The installation of a different tool, mold, die, or control program in a production machine (such as a lathe or milling machine, injection molding machine, or painting system).
Constraint	Anything that limits a system from achieving higher performance or throughput.
Contingency Planning	Planning for actions to mitigate risks.
Continuous Flow Production	Production where pieces are completed one at a time in a continuous sequence. Each process makes only the one piece that the next process needs, and the transfer batch size is one.
Continuous Improvement Process (CIP)	The never-ending process of improving quality and / or eliminating waste within an organization.
Control Chart	A statistical tool tracking a process to ensure it functions to produce output within established limits.
Control Element	A specific process variable which must be controlled in an experiment.
Counter measures	Immediate actions taken to bring performance that is tracking below expectations back into the proper trend.

Glossary

Counterclockwise flow	Traditional manufacturing cell layout drives the flow of material, and the motion of people, from right to left, or counterclockwise (said to originate from the design of tools with chucks on the left side, making it easier for right-handed people to load from right to left).
Covariance	A measure of the strength of correlation between two or more random variables.
Current State Map	A schematic illustrating a current process.

Curtain effect	A method that permits the uninterrupted flow of production regardless of external process location or cycle time. Normally used when product must leave the cell for processing through equipment that cannot be put into the cell. (i.e. heat treat, curing oven, plating, wave solder) Curtain quantities are established using the following formula:
	    Per unit Cycle Time of Curtain Process / Takt Time = Curtain
	       Quantity.

Cycle Time	The time required to complete one cycle of an operation.
D	
Daily Management	Attention each day to those issues concerned with the normal operation of a business.
Dependent Events	Events that occur only after a previous event.
Discount Rate	The rate of interest assumed to represent the current cost of money.
E	
EOQ (Economic Order Quantity)	EOQ is the right amount of an item to order to minimize the trade-off between ordering costs and the carrying cost of inventory.
Error Proofing	Designing a cause of potential failure, or a hazard to

	safety, out of a product or process.
Every Part Every	'Every Product Every (hours, day, week, month)' indicates the flexibility to produce whatever the customer needs. For instance, Every Product Every day would indicate that changeovers for all products required can be performed each day and the products can be supplied to the customer.
F	
Flow	Movement of product continuously from raw material to finished goods through a production system that acted as one long conveyor.
Flow Chart	A schematic chart that illustrates a process, sometimes showing the 'as is' and 'to be' processes for comparison, identifying wasteful steps.
Flow Production	Production designed to pull product from operation to operation in the smallest increment (ideally one piece at a time).
Functional Layout	The practice of grouping machines or activities by type of operation performed.
Future State Map	A blueprint for a 'to be' process.
G	
Gain Sharing	An approach to providing incentives for team success, such as a share of the cost reduction or revenue increase.
Gemba	Japanese word for 'real place,' the actual shop floor where production occurs.
Gembutsu	Japanese for 'actual thing' or 'actual product,' the tools, materials, machines, parts, and fixtures that are the focus of kaizen activity.
Genjitsu	Japanese for 'the facts' or 'the reality,' applied to the shop floor / the business.
Genchi Genbutsu	Japanese for 'see for yourself,' without relying on reports from a distance.

Glossary

Greenfield	A new production facility.
H	
Hanedashi	A device for automatically off-loading a work piece from a machine when it is finished at that machine, essential for a 'Chaku-Chaku' line.
Heijunka	Japanese for 'leveling.' The concept is applied to production in small batches at final assembly, enabling JIT and other lean practices. This is particularly beneficial on a mixed-model production line.
High Performance Teams	Teams that perform complex tasks correctly and quickly.
Histogram	A chart that displays a series of metrics (x axis) according to the frequency of each (y axis) in order to understand variations. With enough data points this may result in a standard curve.
Hoshin Kanri / Hoshin Planning	A tool for linking long-term goals to daily activities by clarifying strategies that support the goals, critical success factors that enable the strategies, and core competencies that make the critical success factors possible. Generally created by the senior management team and aligning people at all levels. (Hoshin Kanri means 'Direction Management')
I	
Ijo-kanri	Being able to see and quickly take action to correct abnormalities.
Insource	To make a previously purchased part in one's own factory. This should be done if it can be made for less (including the costs of quality) and excess capacity exists and/or to ensure the reliability of supply.
Integrated Product Development	Refers to processes that bring engineering, marketing, financial, and production experts together to design and introduce new products.

J	
Jidoka	'Autonomation' allows a machine to stop instantly if it detects defects.
Jishuken	Lower level management driven focus identifying kaizen opportunities.
Just-in-Time (JIT)	A system for producing and delivering the right items to the right place at the right time, in the right amounts. 'Just-in-Time' requires focus on balanced flow, pull procedures, standard work, and Takt time.
K	
Kaizen	Japanese for little fixes, generally applied to team efforts of a few days (Kaizen Blitz) to rapidly analyze and improve processes or sub- processes.
Kanban	A signaling device, often 'low tech,' which orders parts to be produced and delivered in a pull system.
L	
Lead Time	The time a customer must wait for an order to be filled. This applies also to a process on a production line waiting for work pieces to arrive.
Lean	Business processes requiring less human effort, capital investment, floor space, materials, and time in all aspects of operation.
M	
Mistake Proofing	Any equipment or procedure change to an operation that helps the operator reduce or eliminate errors.
Muda	Japanese for waste, applied to anything that interferes with the value stream.
Multi-Skilled Worker	Associates at any organizational level with diverse skills, providing flexibility in a production process.
Mura	Japanese for unevenness, as in an unbalanced production line, solved through kanbans.
Muri	Japanese for overburden, unreasonableness or absurdity.
N	

Glossary

Non-Value Added	Activities that add no customer demanded value to a product or service.
O	
One Piece Flow	Operators transfer each item individually to the next process step.
Operating Cycle	The number of days from the time money is spent until it is collected, from the purchases that go into inventory to the collection of receivables.
Operating Expenses	The money required for the organization to be in the business, making product and supporting the operation.
Outsource	To purchase a part externally that was previously made in house. This is usually done to reduce costs, but might also make sense if an outside fiorm can improve on the quality.
Overproduction	Producing more, sooner or faster than is required by the next process.
P	
PDCA (Plan, Do, Check, Act)	A logical sequence for fixing any problem, unfortunately frequently forgotten. PLAN: Analyze the problem and develop an appropriate plan of action, specifying who, what, where, when, and how and the expected benefits. DO: Perform the actions. CHECK: Review the measurements to ensure benefits are on track. ACT: Redirect efforts as necessary.
Pareto Chart	A vertical bar graph showing the frequency of causes of error in descending order, generally indicating that a few causes are most frequent (the 80/20 rule).
Peer Group	Firms with similar assets, operations, and markets.
Perfection	An unattainable goal approached by optimizing value-added activities
Poka-Yoke	Error / mistake proofing using devices or procedures to prevent inefficient or unsafe actions. For

	examples, in-line weighing would prevent out of spec parts from proceeding to the next step, and safety gates would keep hands out of dangerous machines.
Process	Operations that transform material (or paperwork) from input to finished product.
Process Kaizen	Improvements made at an individual process or in a specific area. Sometimes called 'point kaizen.'
Process Reengineering	Integrated restructuring of operations to improve effectiveness and efficiency.
Process Map	A visual representation of the sequential flow of a process to identify opportunities for improvement.
Processing Time	The time a product is actually being worked on in a machine or work area
Pull	A system of cascading production and delivery instructions from downstream to upstream activities in which the upstream supplier waits until the downstream customer signals a need.
Pull System	Product is pulled through a process, starting with the end user. A sale triggers production of another unit, production of the unit triggers suppliers to send sub-assemblies or raw materials, and so on. Very little excess inventory is created.
Push System	Product is pushed into a process, regardless of whether it is needed, often creating excess inventory.
Q	
Quality Function Deployment (QFD)	A visual decision-making tool for cross-functional project teams that focuses on the voice of the customer, addresses product performance targets and trade-offs, and develops consensus and team commitment to product specifications. QFD reduces expensive rework as projects near launch.
Quality Management	The organizations, practices, and tools that make it possible to plan, manufacture, and deliver quality

Glossary

	products / services.
Quick Changeover	Rapid change of tooling / fixtures when multiple products run on the same machine.
Queue Time	The time a product spends in a line awaiting the next design, order processing, or fabrication step.
R	
RACI	Responsible-Accountable-Consulted-Informed – descriptions of Roles and Responsibilities, to be analyzed and clarified as needed
Reengineering	Fundamentally revising integrated processes throughout a company to improve quality and efficiently.
Resource Utilization	Using a resource for any purpose (preferably to add value).
S	
Sensei	A master / teacher who helps implement lean or Six Sigma practices. The term was originally applied in Oriental martial arts.
Sequential Changeover	Changeover / setup of machines within Takt time so that multiple products can be made on the same line without interrupting the flow.
Single Minute Exchange of Dies (SMED)	Concept of rapid machine changeover / setup to keep production flowing with minimal downtime when multiple products run on the same machine. Ideally changeover would be instantaneous and would not interfere with continuous flow.
Single-Piece Flow	A production process in which products are pulled through production one complete product at a time.
Standards	Accepted norms, often set by regulatory organizations.
Standard Work	A precise description of each work activity specifying cycle time, Takt time, the work sequence of specific tasks, and the minimum inventory of parts on hand needed to conduct the activity.
Standard Work in	The minimum amount of material for a given product

Process	which must be in process at any time to ensure proper flow of the operation.
Standardization	Use of uniform methods and processes to ensure uniform output
Supplier Partnership	Close working relationship with a supplier to gain mutual benefits, such as more revenue or less cost through better designs, logistics, etc.
System Kaizen	Improvement aimed at an entire value stream
Sub-Optimization	Taking action to improve efficiency in one area that negatively impacts the efficiency of another area even more.
T	
Takt Time	The available production time divided by the rate of customer demand. For example, if customers demand 480 automobiles per 480 minute shift, Takt time is one minute.
Team Oriented Problem Solving	Many tools and techniques of continuous improvement are designed to help teams focus on and resolve problems.
Theory of Constraints	A lean management philosophy focused on removing constraints to increase throughput and decrease inventory / expenses.
Throughput Time	The time required by a process to complete its value-adding activities.
Total Productive Maintenance (TPM)	A disciplined integration of maintenance schedules with production schedules in order to prevent unplanned down time and gain optimum run time from every significant machine.
Toyota Production System (TPS)	A manufacturing philosophy that relentlessly attacks waste while improving quality and shortening work cycles
V	
Value	The right product (defined by the customer) at the right price (defined by the competition).

Glossary

Value-Added Analysis	Analysis of activities to determine which add value from the customer's perspective in order to eliminate non-value adding activities (wasted effort).
Value Stream / Value Chain	The progressive sequential activities that add value to a product –material management, fabrication, logistics, etc. – from raw material to finished product.
Value Stream Mapping	Creating a schematic of how material gains value as it moves through an operation in order to identify opportunities to eliminate waste.
Vertical Teams	Teams that include employees from multiple organizational levels.
Visual Control	Information, parts, and tools displayed for instant understanding of the process or system status.
W	
Waste	Anything produced that has no value; any use of resources that produces nothing of value.
Work in Progress (WIP)	Product or inventory in various stages of completion throughout the plant, once released as raw material to the floor and before becoming finished goods ready for shipment.
Work Sequence	The order in which work steps occur.
World Class	An overused term meaning 'done as well as the best in the world.'
Y	
Yokoten	Duplicating the results of a kaizen event.
Yield	Per cent of material and labor input that becomes acceptable finished product.

www.ingramcontent.com/pod-product-compliance
Lightning Source LLC
Chambersburg PA
CBHW080245180526
45167CB00006B/2422